SECONDARY CAUSE OF DEATH

SECONDARY CAUSE OF DEATH

by Peter Gordon

JOSEF WEINBERGER PLAYS

LONDON

Secondary Cause of Death
First published in 1999
by Josef Weinberger Ltd
(pka Warner/Chappell Plays Ltd)
12-14 Mortimer Street
London W1T 3JJ
www.josef-weinberger.com
general.info@jwmail.co.uk

ISBN   0 85676 243 1 (10 digit)
        978 0 85676 243 7 (13 digit)

To Janice
with love and thanks for her help and encouragement

CHARACTERS

LADY ISADORA POLLOCK

COUNT PUCHLIK OF PUSZCZYKOWO, *a Polish Gentleman*

COLONEL CHARLES CRADDOCK, *retired*

CAPTAIN HENRIETTA WOOLMER-CARDINGTON, *an ATS Officer*

CYNTHIA MAPLE

CARDEW LONGFELLOW, *a Thespian (played by same actor as*
COLONEL CRADDOCK)

MARTHA ARMSTRONG, *Housekeeper*

LILY TUTHILL, *Cook*

INSPECTOR PRATT

NURSE ANN PARSLEY

The action of the play takes place in the library/sitting room
of a country manor house in early Spring 1939.

ACT ONE

Scene One: Afternoon
                  That evening

Scene Two: Later the same evening
                  Fifteen minutes later

ACT TWO

Scene One: Several minutes later
                  Later that evening
                  Several minutes later

Scene Two: The following morning

ACT ONE

Scene One

The action takes place in 1939 in the library/sitting room of Bagshot House. The entire room has the effect of wood panelling. Upstage right is a door which leads to the dining room. Centre is a door which leads to the hallway. To the right of the door is a bookcase. Another bookcase is along the upstage left wall. Just down from this bookcase is a secret door, set into the panelling, which leads to a passageway. Down left is a slightly raised hearth on which is a fireplace companion set, indicating the presence of a fireplace in the corner of the room. A brass scuttle for storage of logs is positioned by the hearth. The room is furnished with a large settee, down right, and two chairs down left near the fireplace. To the right of the settee is a small table, draped with a cloth, on which is positioned a brass candlestick. Behind the settee, hidden from the audience by the settee and table, is a low level entrance hatch in the wall, just large enough to allow secret entrance by an actor. There is a sideboard in the corner up left, on which are a number of decanters and glasses, a wooden cigar box and an oil lamp.

As the curtain opens there are two people in the room. LADY ISADORA POLLOCK *is sitting on the chair, down left, reading a book. She is an elegant woman in her forties.* COUNT PUCHLIK OF PUSZCZYKOWO (*a Polish Gentleman*) *is browsing the bookcase on the upstage wall. He is dressed as he believes an English Gentleman should dress. He speaks rather bad English but in a formal way which he considers will help his portrayal of a well-to-do Englishman. He has a very pronounced East European accent. He carries a dictionary around with him for reference purposes and has a monocle which he occasionally wears as he refers to the dictionary.*

COLONEL CHARLES CRADDOCK *enters from the hall, followed by* CAPTAIN HENRIETTA WOOLMER-CARDINGTON. CHARLES *is retired and in his sixties. He is dressed in a tweed jacket and has a confident but blustering manner.* HENRIETTA *is a relatively young Army Territorial Service Captain dressed in uniform. She is obviously from a family of breeding but she is rather school-girlish and endearingly stupid. She has great difficulty in pronouncing the letter 'r'.*

CHARLES	This way, this way. Just show you into the old . . . erm, (*Lost for words.*) what's name . . .
HENRIETTA	Oh, absolutely, yes.(*Looking around enthusiastically.*)
PUCHLIK	(*looking up*) Is called library.
CHARLES	Pardon, old boy?
PUCHLIK	Is called library.
HENRIETTA	(*with a spark of recognition*) So it is. I do believe you're right . . . it is. By golly, yes. (*Thoughtful.*) We had one of these at Roedean you know. Me and the other girls would lark about in there. Tremendous fun.
PUCHLIK	Library. A room where books are kept. My English is very excellent, yes? (*Holding his dictionary aloft.*) I use dictionary. He is my friend.
CHARLES	Quite right, old boy, jolly good. (*Confidentially to* HENRIETTA *by way of explanation.*) Foreign sort of fellow if you get my meaning.
PUCHLIK	(*to* HENRIETTA) Count Pavel Puchlik of Puszczykowo at your most humblest of services.
HENRIETTA	(*offering her hand*) Jolly nice I'm sure. Captain Henrietta Woolmer-Cardington, Army Territorial Service.
PUCHLIK	Is nice to make your acquaintance, Captain.

HENRIETTA	That's the Hampshire Woolmer-Cardington's, not the Essex. People get us terribly confused. (*Joking.*) Don't know why . . . *they're* quite bright.
PUCHLIK	Hampshire or Essex, is still very nice. Is very cold snap we are having at the moment, I believe.
HENRIETTA	Oh absolutely. Wouldn't be surprised if we didn't have a spot of snow later on.
PUCHLIK	In Poland we have the very bad snows up to the neck. You do not have it so very bad here I think.
ISADORA	The Count is infatuated with discussing the vagaries of our weather. He believes that it makes him seem very English.
CHARLES	(*moving towards* ISADORA) Ah, Isadora. Thought you were going out riding?
ISADORA	(*laughing*) Not after I heard the Count's weather forecast at breakfast. I was expecting monsoons and tidal waves at the very least.
CHARLES	Tidal waves? Nasty pieces o' work. Did I ever tell you about the time I was in India? I got hit by the most enormous affair you've ever seen in your life? Must have been ten feet high . . . probably nearer forty when I think of it.
PUCHLIK	You told us story over dinner last night, Colonel. Was very amusing.
ISADORA	(*laughing*) And you told us again over breakfast this morning.
PUCHLIK	Was not so amusing.

CHARLES Did I really? Dashed if I can remember! In fact, I can't even remember the story now!

(ISADORA *rises*.)

ISADORA Let me introduce myself. (*Offering her hand to* HENRIETTA.) Lady Isadora Pollock.

HENRIETTA (*moving to* ISADORA *and taking her offered hand*) Jolly nice to meet you. Knew a couple of Pollocks at school actually. Absolutely top sort of people.

(ISADORA *indicates that* HENRIETTA *should sit in the chair next to her. They both sit*.)

ISADORA What brings you to Bagshot House, Henrietta?

HENRIETTA Oh, just on a bit of army whatnot. GHQ seem to think Bagshot House may be of value as an Ops centre if Herr Hitler starts any funny business. They sent me on a bit of a recce. Can't say too much, all a bit hush hush.

PUCHLIK (*moving down in front of the settee*) The storm clouds are gathering over Europe, Captain.

HENRIETTA Are they? Wouldn't really know actually. Haven't had the chance to see the full forecast myself.

PUCHLIK I am using one of your English metaphors.

HENRIETTA Are you really? (*Giggling*.) Sounds terribly clever!

PUCHLIK (*waving his dictionary*) A figure of speech in which word or phrase is used in order to imply a resemblance.

HENRIETTA Gosh!

CHARLES   (*moving down towards* PUCHLIK) Just let that
                 Hitler blighter try anything, that's all I can say.
                 We'll soon show him the way back to Berlin.
                 Like we did Kaiser Bill and his cronies.

HENRIETTA   Absolutely. We'll give him jolly well what for
                 . . . and a bit of a comeuppance to boot.

CHARLES   Well said. Like the cut of your jib. I'll have a
                 drink to that. Anybody care to join me?

                 (CHARLES *moves to the sideboard and during
                 the course of the following conversation helps
                 himself to a couple of drinks.*)

ISADORA   Not at present, thank you.

PUCHLIK   (*sitting on the settee*) I will have one of your
                 Scotland malted whiskies.

CHARLES   Scotch? You're catching on fast, old boy.
                 Henrietta?

HENRIETTA   Just a small sherry if poss. Jolly old report to
                 write later. Don't want to get squiffy-eyed!

CHARLES   Quite unusual to find a young gal like you in
                 uniform.

HENRIETTA   Oh, there's been a Woolmer-Cardington in the
                 army for centuries. Daddy was a bit
                 disappointed when I turned out to be a girl.
                 There was a Woolmer-Cardington at Waterloo,
                 actually. He took part in that famous cavalry
                 charge of the Scots Greys.

CHARLES   (*moving down behind* HENRIETTA) Did he really
                 . . . there's a thing! Good show.

HENRIETTA   Not so good actually. He was a Colonel in the
                 infantry and his horse just got a bit caught up
                 in all the excitement. Bit of an embarrassment.

CHARLES   Ah . . . (*Moving back to the sideboard.*) . . .
               bad luck.

HENRIETTA   I'm more in communications, that sort of thing.

ISADORA   I hope your report won't stop you from joining
               us in a little adventure mystery this evening.
               I've even persuaded the Count to join in.

HENRIETTA   Oh, gosh! Hide and seek, sardines, that sort of
               thing is it? I used to be pretty good at that in
               the dorm.

ISADORA   Oh, it's far more sophisticated than that.

CHARLES   (*taking glasses of Scotch to* PUCHLIK *and
               sherry to* HENRIETTA) Just a harmless bit of fun.
               When I was bequeathed this big old pile I
               turned it into a bit of an exclusive hotel affair.
               Just the occasional guest, top drawer people,
               none of your riff-raff. Rather hoped some of the
               chaps from the club might pop along
               occasionally but it didn't work out. Anyway,
               we're a bit isolated here so I had to think of
               something a bit different. Heard of a woman
               down in the village who does re-enactment
               affairs . . . famous murder mysteries and all that
               type of thing. Bit rich considering what
               happened here a while back but it seems to get
               the punters in.

ISADORA   When I read about these mysteries in the *Times*
               I was intrigued. They're organised by a woman
               called Cynthia Maple.

CHARLES   Dreadful woman. Still, she seems to know what
               she's about I suppose.

               (CYNTHIA'S *voice is heard from the hall.*)

CYNTHIA   (*off*) That's the way, Mrs Tuthill. Kick on.
               Dinner no later than eight, otherwise we'll fall
               way behind schedule.

CHARLES   Here she comes. Time I made myself scarce.

(CHARLES *is terrified of* CYNTHIA *and gulps the last mouthful from his glass and attempts to escape into the dining room. He is not quick enough and is pulled up short by the entrance of* CYNTHIA *from the hall. She is a middle-aged woman with an overbearing, brusque and caustic manner. She wears a tweed skirt and baggy cardigan.*)

CYNTHIA   Colonel! Just the man I was looking for. Need a quick word.

CHARLES   Rather thought you might.

CYNTHIA   (*glancing around the room*) Good afternoon, Lady Pollock . . . Count Puchlik.

(PUCHLIK *stands and clicks his heels together before sitting again.* CYNTHIA *notices* HENRIETTA *and marches over to her, offering her hand.* HENRIETTA *stands.*)

Haven't met. Cynthia Maple. Pleased to meet you. (*Pumping her hand up and down furiously.*)

HENRIETTA   (*wincing*) Henrietta Woolmer-Cardington.

CYNTHIA   (*releasing her hand*) Need to firm up that handshake, my girl, if you're going to get anywhere. Bit of a limp lettuce feel at the moment.

HENRIETTA   (*backing away behind the chair*) Gosh . . . have to do some exercises or something. Thing is though, I don't think I'll be able to join in with your game.

CYNTHIA   (*scowling*) Murder is never a game, Captain! Serious business.

HENRIETTA

Yes, I suppose it is. I'm sure it all sounds like ripping fun but I have work to do, bit pushed for time.

(*Seeing that* CYNTHIA *is occupied,* CHARLES *tries to sneak to the hall door.*)

CYNTHIA

Nonsense. You'll just have to make time.

(*Without waiting for a reply,* CYNTHIA *marches back to* CHARLES.)

Not about to shoot off, Colonel?

CHARLES

No, absolutely not. Wouldn't have dreamed of it. Just thought I might have another drink.

(CHARLES *tries to skirt around* CYNTHIA *to get to the drinks cabinet.*)

CYNTHIA

How many have you had?

CHARLES

Today? Two . . . small ones. Unimaginably small as it happens . . . minute . . . you'd hardly notice them.

CYNTHIA

No more for you until dinner then. Now, the thing is, Colonel, you must impress on Mrs Tuthill the utmost importance of serving dinner at precisely twenty hundred hours. Do I make myself clear?

CHARLES

Quite clear. Message received and understood.

CYNTHIA

If the re-enactment is to work effectively, timing is vital. (*Turning to the others.*) Colonel Craddock has a starring role in this evening's mystery. A little invention of mine. 'The Mysterious Case of the Identical Twins.'

CHARLES

Rather not be involved, old girl.

CYNTHIA What nonsense. Lady Pollock, you will play the role of an American lady of rather dubious morals.

ISADORA How exciting.

CYNTHIA Yes, I'm sure you'll manage it very convincingly. Count Puchlik will be a member of Parliament. Captain Woolmer-Cardington will serve nicely as herself I think. Anything else may be over-ambitious. I will have character cards prepared for you all in good time. (*Walking briskly to the hall door.*) Now then, Colonel. Let's go and speak to your staff.

CHARLES Right, absolutely . . . whatever you say.

CYNTHIA Come along then. No time to waste.

CHARLES On my way, old girl, lead on.

(CYNTHIA *exits followed by* CHARLES.)

HENRIETTA (*stunned*) Gosh!

ISADORA I know. She does seem a bit of a tartar at first meeting.

(PUCHLIK *looks puzzled and consults his dictionary.*)

HENRIETTA I thought my CO was a bit of a formidable type but she wouldn't hold a candle to her. She reminds me of my old hockey captain, she was a bit of a tyrant . . . all shin guards and teeth.

ISADORA Apparently Miss Maple's sister is rather famous. A sort of amateur sleuth. That's where she gets many of the ideas for her mysteries. They had such a terrible tragedy here . . . had you heard?

HENRIETTA   Ghastly business from what I've been told.
             Rather gives me the creeps.

PUCHLIK   Excuse. Why do you call her deposit on tooth?
             Is this same as pain on neck?

ISADORA   I'm sorry, Count, you've rather lost me.

PUCHLIK   (*consulting his dictionary closely*) Tartar. Is
             deposit on teeth.

ISADORA   Ah . . . wrong sort of tartar. It's one of those
             funny words that can mean different things.

HENRIETTA   I've always had a lot of trouble with those
             sorts of words myself. I mean, there are so
             many of them aren't there . . . like . . . like er . . .
             well, like banana for example.

PUCHLIK   Banana?

HENRIETTA   Absolutely. You see, I might say "I feel like a
             banana" meaning I want to eat one, not that I
             actually feel like one . . . you know, like how a
             banana might feel . . . sad or something like
             that.

             (*Both* ISADORA *and* PUCHLIK *stare at her in
             amazement. She shuffles uncomfortably.*)

             That wasn't a good example was it? I'll think of
             another one, shall I?

ISADORA   (*sitting*) I think the Count already understands
             what we mean.

HENRIETTA   Do you? Jolly good . . . bit of a relief actually
             . . . couldn't think of any more.

             (*There is a sudden commotion from the hall.*
             CARDEW LONGFELLOW'S *voice is heard off.*
             CARDEW *is* CHARLES'S *double* (*played by the*

same actor). Although he looks like CHARLES
*he has a loud, booming and haughty
theatrical voice. He is talking to* MARTHA, *the
housekeeper, also off. She has a working class
accent.*)

CARDEW   (*off*) Madam, I seek liquid refreshment. I
                wonder if you might kindly inform me from
                whence such sustenance may be appropriated.

MARTHA   (*off*) What's that you're after, sir?

CARDEW   (*off*) A drink, madam, a drink.

MARTHA   (*off*) Oh, I get you now, sir. I could make you a
                nice cup of tea if you'd like.

CARDEW   I was anticipating a beverage of a more
                invigorating, not to say intoxicating, nature. In
                short, my good lady, alcohol.

MARTHA   (*off*) Oh, you'd best try the library then, sir.
                Just through the door there. On the sideboard
                in the corner.

CARDEW   (*off*) Thank you for your trouble, madam. My
                most humble and grateful thanks.

MARTHA   (*off*) Thank *you*, sir.

                (CARDEW *enters from the hall. In contrast to*
                CHARLES, *he wears a cape rather than a jacket
                and a cravat rather than a tie. Every
                mannerism is larger than life. As he enters, he
                notices the others in the room.*)

CARDEW   Ah. A social convocation. Greetings to one and
                to all.

HENRIETTA   (*uncertain, moving towards* CARDEW) Oh, yes,
                greetings to one. Henrietta Woolmer-

Cardington. May I introduce Lady Isadora
Pollock . . .

ISADORA   Sir.

HENRIETTA   And Count Puchlik.

(*The* COUNT *stands and clicks his heels
together smartly.*)

CARDEW   My pleasure, sir. Allow me to introduce myself.
Cardew Longfellow, late of the Hackney Empire
and more latterly the Oldham Coliseum.
Pantomime and music hall review a speciality.

PUCHLIK   Is nice to make your acquaintance, Mister
Longfellow. (*Sitting again.*) Is very cold snap
we are having at the moment, I believe.

CARDEW   It is indeed, sir. (*Theatrically.*) "The way was
long, the wind was cold, The Minstrel was
infirm and old; his wither'd cheek and tresses
grey, Seem'd to have known a better day".

(*The others are rather startled, not knowing
how to react.*)

(*by way of explanation*) Sir Walter Scott.

HENRIETTA   (*finally*) Well, bravo for that, Sir Walter . . .
well done!

CARDEW   This particular minstrel comes in search of
refreshment and I spy it close to hand. (*Moving
to the sideboard.*) I see that you (*Indicating*
HENRIETTA *and* PUCHLIK.) are momentarily
replete, but perhaps you may wish to join me,
dear Lady.

(*Over* CARDEW's *following speeches,* PUCHLIK
uses his dictionary with increasingly furious

desperation as he tries to keep track of what is being said.)

ISADORA   Not at present thank you. May I ask what brings you to Bagshot House, Mister Longfellow. If you don't mind me remarking upon it, you do have an uncanny resemblance to Colonel Craddock.

HENRIETTA   (*moving towards* CARDEW) Yes indeed. When you walked through the door I thought for a moment that I was seeing the Colonel's double . . . when in fact I was! Pretty spooky really.

CARDEW   I am employed by a Miss Cynthia Maple on a temporary engagement of one weekend's duration. Tonight being the opening night as it were.

ISADORA   Oh, super. Now I see . . . "The Case of the Identical Twins". Already the plot thickens.

HENRIETTA   And we haven't even got a plot yet!

(*There is a knock at the dining room door.*)

Oh, I say, there's someone at the door. Do come in.

(*They all wait for several seconds in expectation. No one enters and there is another knock at the door.*)

CARDEW   (*booming*) Enter those who wait without.

(LILY *peers through the doorway. She wears a cook's outfit. She has a strong regional accent.*)

LILY   (*hesitant*) Enter those without what?

CARDEW   A mere figure of speech, Madam. I merely bade you cross yonder portal. How may we be of assistance?

LILY   (*moving further into the room*) It's just that I were looking for Martha. 'Ave you seen 'er?

PUCHLIK   Martha is homekeeper, yes?

LILY   'Ousekeeper.

PUCHLIK   Is same thing I think.

CARDEW   I believe I may be of some minuscule assistance. But moments ago I had occasion to orally articulate with the lady to whom you refer. She was embarking on an excursive expedition of a logistical nature I believe.

LILY   I'm sorry, I don't get you.

HENRIETTA   Neither do I, actually.

CARDEW   She was going shopping.

LILY   Oh, right. Why didn't you say? It's just I was after some 'elp. I'm in a bit of a tiz an' I don't right know what to do.

ISADORA   Anything we can assist with, perhaps?

LILY   I shouldn't think so. Does anybody know anything about rabbits?

CARDEW   Ah, rabbits. As it happens, some years ago, I fell into the acquaintance of a gentleman who could perform the most exquisite magic with rabbits.

LILY   Do you 'appen to know 'ow long he did 'em for . . . in a casserole.

CARDEW	He was a conjurer, Madam.
LILY	Oh I see. (*Clearly not seeing at all. There is a moment's pause.*) So you don't know 'ow long he did 'em?
CARDEW	(*exasperated*) He was a magician.
	(LILY *still looks blank.*)
	He did tricks!
LILY	Oh, I see. Why didn't you say? Don't suppose anybody else knows?
HENRIETTA	Afraid not. I'm an officer. I'm not really expected to know much about anything.
LILY	It's just that Miss Maple insists it 'as to be rabbit . . . and I don't do rabbit. I do cows, sheep and pigs but not rabbit . . . there's not enough meat on 'em.
	(CYNTHIA *enters from the hall carrying some sheets of paper.*)
CYNTHIA	I have character cards for Lady Pollock and . . .
	(*She is stopped in her tracks when she sees* CARDEW.)
	What are you doing in here, Mr Longfellow?
CARDEW	I am currently engaged in discourse with this lady. I was reviewing the relative merits of a range of butchered comestibles, though I must confess that I am somewhat mystified as to how the conversation came about.
LILY	It's because I'm the cook.

CYNTHIA   Then perhaps you should be in the kitchen . . . cooking!

LILY   Yes, I suppose so. I'll just 'ave to wait 'til Martha gets back. Don't know 'ow long she'll be though. Might not be ready for eight.

CYNTHIA   You'd better be!

(LILY *exits into the dining room.*)

Dreadful woman. (*Turning her attention back to* CARDEW.) Now, I was intending that you stay concealed until the appropriate moment. Your premature entrance may affect certain elements of my plot. Not good.

CARDEW   My apologies, madam. Upon perambulatory ingress to the room I was unaware of prior occupation. I will leave you now and prepare myself for the forthcoming performance. Until we meet again I wish you all a brief but fond farewell.

(CARDEW *sweeps from the room with a flourish of arms.*)

HENRIETTA   Strange sort of fellow! Do you think he might be a bit doolally?

CYNTHIA   He's an actor . . . they're all doolally. He has the added advantage of being remarkably cheap. Now, as I was about to say, I have the character cards for you, Lady Isadora and for you, Count. If you'd like to come upstairs with me I have some suitable clothes prepared for you. As for you, Captain, I've had further thoughts so you'd better come along as well and we'll see if we can equip you.

ISADORA   Please do join in with us, Henrietta. I'm sure your boring old work will wait and I just know that this evening will be truly memorable.

HENRIETTA   Well, it does seem like a bit of a wheeze.
             Suppose it wouldn't do any harm. Rather like
             dressing up actually, that's why I joined the
             A.T.S.

ISADORA   Then we are all yours, Miss Maple. Do with us
             as you wish.(*Standing and moving centre
             stage.*) Would you care to take my arm, Count?

PUCHLIK   (m*oving to take* ISADORA's *arm*) Would be my
             delight, Lady Isadora.

ISADORA   Then lead on, Miss Maple.

             (*They all exit into the hallway, leaving the
             hall door open. The lights fade briefly to
             denote passage of time, then rise again.* LILY's
             voice is heard off in the hall.)

LILY   (*off*) I'll show you into the library, Inspector,
             then I'll fetch the Colonel for you. Just through
             there, sir . . . that's it . . .

             (INSPECTOR PRATT *wanders down the hall,
             passing the open door way as he move across
             it from stage left to stage right. As he passes
             the open door he turns his head to the left,
             looking slightly bewildered, before he passes
             out of sight. A few seconds later a crash of
             buckets and falling crockery is heard.*)

             No, sir, that's a cupboard . . . that's it . . .
             through there.

             (INSPECTOR PRATT *enters from the hall. He is an
             inept, clumsy, walking disaster area. He wears
             his trademark overcoat and a hat. After
             entering, he moves to the centre of the room
             and looks around knowingly.*)

PRATT   Oh, yes. I remember it very well.

(He suddenly pulls a revolver from his coat pocket, crouches and pretends to fire several shots around the room from the revolver. He smiles, satisfied with himself, replacing the revolver in his pocket. Seeing the drinks on the sideboard he glances around to make sure that he is alone, then moves to the sideboard. Noticing that there is a glass there with drink still in it, he picks up the glass and wipes the top of it with his sleeve. He wanders across the room, sipping the drink and looking around the room. His attention is caught by an area of floor near the dining room door and he bends slightly to examine it, his back to the hall door. CHARLES *enters from the hall but* PRATT *is lost in thought and does not hear him.* CHARLES, *at a loss, clears his throat loudly.* PRATT *stands bolt upright, swiftly finishes the drink and thrusts the empty glass guiltily into his coat pocket before removing his hat and turning rapidly to face* CHARLES.)*

CHARLES (*looking at* PRATT *in horror*) Good, Lord . . . I don't believe it. It's you!

PRATT Colonel Craddock, we meet again. It's been some time. A lot of water has passed under the hedge since then. Oh, yes, a long time indeed.

(During the following couple of speeches, PRATT *offers his hand to* CHARLES. *As* CHARLES *moves to shake hands,* PRATT *suddenly realises his hand may not be very clean after the episode with the glass. He withdraws his hand, inspecting it and trying to dry it on his coat, leaving* CHARLES *embarrassed with an outstretched hand. Finally Pratt finishes drying his hand but by then has forgotten about the handshake and wanders down behind the settee.* CHARLES *withdraws his hand sheepishly.)*

CHARLES Must say I was rather hoping for a lot longer.

PRATT   Understandable, Colonel, in the circumstances. The very regrettable and unfortunate circumstances if I may say so.

CHARLES   Sorry, old boy. I wouldn't like you to take offence.

PRATT   (*in surprise*) Don't worry, Colonel, your fence is quite safe. I have no need of it.

CHARLES   My fence!

PRATT   Exactly

CHARLES   Why should I think you'd want that, old boy?

PRATT   Exactly what I was asking myself. It seemed strange that you were preoccupied with it.

CHARLES   (*baffled*) Look I don't wish to seem impolite, old boy, but is there any particular reason for this visit? I assume it's not social.

PRATT   Regrettably I only have time for anti-social visits, Colonel Craddock. The weight of responsibility lies heavily on those of us charged with upholding the law of the land.

CHARLES   Well, I hope it's not about that other business. I mean it's been three years. I'm trying to forget. I'd rather not talk about it, old chap. If it's all the same to you?

PRATT   Don't worry, Colonel. I fully respect your feelings. A tragic affair.

CHARLES   Yes it was.

PRATT   Such a pity your wife found out.

CHARLES   Look, old boy. Do you have to?

PRATT Not another word. Thoughtless of me.
(*Strolling across towards the dining room door and gazing thoughtfully at the floor.*) I see you got the blood stain out of the carpet.

CHARLES Really, old boy!

PRATT If I'm not mistaken, this used to be the dining room. I never forget a detail.

CHARLES As it happens this used to be the billiard room.

PRATT (*turning and leaning casually on the door frame with his back to the door*) Yes, as I thought. Total carnage. Many an investigator would have fled the scene in horror, Colonel, but not me. I have no fear.

(NURSE PARSLEY *appears silently at the dining room door. She is young, attractive and flirts cheekily with* CHARLES *at every opportunity. She wears a nurse's cape. In one hand she carries a medical bag but in the other she carries raised scissors. She stops in the doorway, blocked by* PRATT *who senses a presence and suddenly spins around. Seeing the scissors, he pleads with arms outstretched.*)

I'll give you anything! Anything you like!

NURSE Well, I'd rather like to get past you, sir, if possible. It's time for me to swap the Colonel's dressing.

PRATT Ah yes, of course.

(PRATT *steps back from the door nonchalantly.* NURSE *walks around him towards* CHARLES.)

(*embarrassed*) Would you like me to leave the room, Colonel?

CHARLES   What for, old boy?

PRATT   (*eyeing* CHARLES *cautiously*) While you and the Nurse swap clothes.

NURSE   No . . . his dressing. It's the Colonel's poultice.

CHARLES   Touch of gout, old boy. Plays up a bit sometimes.

PRATT   Ah, yes, a bout of gout. Just as I thought.

NURSE   (*giggling*) It's the Colonel who plays up, not his gout!

CHARLES   Just a harmless bit of fun. Chap needs a spot of fun now and again.

NURSE   It's time for your medication as well, Colonel.

        (NURSE *puts her bag down on the settee and removes her cape. Standing at the left end of the settee she opens the bag and produces several bottles of pills from it. She starts to sort through them.*)

CHARLES   Dashed nuisance, really. First of all it was the gout, then everything else starts packing up. Getting too old I suppose, that's the trouble. Nothing works as well as it used to.

NURSE   Ooh, I wouldn't say that, Colonel.

CHARLES   Nurse Parsley here sees me right. When I came into all this lot I thought, might as well spoil m'self.

NURSE   You do very well, Colonel. With me looking after you, you'll live to be a hundred.

CHARLES   (*laughing*) With you looking after me, I'll be
          lucky to last another year. What do you say,
          old boy?

NURSE   There's nothing wrong with you that a little bit
          of T.L.C won't put right.

PRATT   Even so, a man of Colonel Craddock's age
          needs to be careful. Oh yes. Heart attack,
          stroke . . . a brain haemorrhoid. I doubt whether
          TCP would be of much use then.

CHARLES   Thanks very much, old boy.

PRATT   Not at all. (*Realising how attractive* NURSE
          PARSLEY *is and preening himself.*) Anyway,
          enough of this. Allow me to introduce myself.
          Pratt. You may have heard of me.

          (PRATT *and* NURSE PARSLEY *shake hands.*)

NURSE   Ann Parsley. Very pleased to meet you. Is there
          any reason I should have heard of you? Are
          you famous?

PRATT   Modesty forbids, Nurse Parsley. But perhaps a
          clue might help. If I tell you that I am a police
          inspector?

NURSE   Oh, you're *that* Pratt. (*Edging slightly away
          from him and returning to her bottles of
          medicine*). Then I have heard of you.

PRATT   (*proudly*) I thought so.

CHARLES   Surprised you're an Inspector after the last
          debacle.

PRATT   (*moving across behind the chairs*) Come,
          come, Colonel. I solved the case single-handed.
          If it hadn't been for the formality of collecting
          evidence . . . (*Scathing.*) which my superior

officers seemed to think was so important . . .
I'd have made arrests within minutes.

CHARLES (*moving to* PRATT) Damn it all, man! You dashed
near got us all killed!

PRATT But thanks to my powers of detection we were
not killed, Colonel. Which brings me to the
crutch of my visit.

CHARLES Crutch?

PRATT (*glancing around the room*) Certainly, Colonel,
where did you leave it?

CHARLES No, you meant crux!

PRATT Did I?

CHARLES Just get on with it, man.

PRATT Get on with what?

CHARLES Why are you here?

PRATT Ah . . . I wondered when we'd get to that.

(PRATT *casually tosses his hat onto the
adjacent chair but misses. He glances at the
chair suspiciously before pulling a notebook
from his pocket.*)

I have grave news, Colonel Craddock.
(*Referring to his notebook.*) Do you remember
a Missus Margaret Craddock.

CHARLES Course I do . . . she's my wife.

PRATT Of course.

CHARLES   She was taken seriously ill after the last lot . . .
                 affected her very badly. Poor old girl. Seemed
                 to blame me for everything.

PRATT   And that is why you may be in danger, Colonel.
                 She has escaped from the safe custard of the
                 asylum.

CHARLES   What!

PRATT   The head of the asylum believes she may have
                 hidden in some bungling fool's car boot.
                 (*Consulting his notes*.) It appears that her
                 escape was discovered on Thursday evening.

CHARLES   Good, God! Heads'll be rolling I hope.

PRATT   Frankly, Colonel, I'm as annoyed as you. She
                 was definitely there on Thursday afternoon . . .
                 I visited her myself. She seemed in good spirits
                 when she walked with me to my car.

CHARLES   So she's on the loose?

PRATT   Have no fear, Colonel. That is what brings me
                 to Bogshot House. I am to be your armed
                 protector until she is returned to the sanitary
                 of the sanctatorium

CHARLES   Armed!

PRATT   (*proudly*) With a gun, Colonel. Do you want to
                 see it?

                 (PRATT *starts to pull a gun from inside his
                 overcoat*.)

CHARLES   No! Put it away! I've seen you with a gun
                 before. (*Backing away protectively towards
                 the* NURSE.) If I were you, my dear, I'd run for
                 my life. (*To* PRATT.) Do the police know you
                 have a gun?

PRATT	I am the police!
CHARLES	I mean someone in authority.
PRATT	I have the authority, Colonel, have no fear.
	(CYNTHIA *enters from the hall.*)
CYNTHIA	Colonel, I must . . . oh, you have visitors?
CHARLES	(*glancing at* PRATT) 'Fraid I have, yes. You've heard of Inspector Pratt?
CYNTHIA	*The* Inspector Pratt?
CHARLES	(*miserably*) Yes.
CYNTHIA	(*face brightening*) I'm so pleased to meet you Inspector.
	(*She shakes* PRATT'S *hand enthusiastically with a vice like grip which makes* PRATT *visibly wilt.*)
	Would you believe that *I* am *Cynthia Maple*?
PRATT	(*massaging his damaged hand*) I have no reason to disbelieve you.
CYNTHIA	No, I mean *Cynthia Maple*. I'm Joan Maple's sister. She helped you solve the last case here. We have so much to talk about, Inspector.
PRATT	Do we?
CYNTHIA	We most certainly do. (*Turning to* NURSE.) And you are?
CHARLES	Haven't you met yet? No, I suppose you haven't. I've employed Nurse Parsley since your last visit.

CYNTHIA   Employed?

CHARLES   Full time nursing care. You can't be too careful.

PRATT   Indeed not.

               (CYNTHIA *glances at* PRATT. *He nods his head knowingly.*)

               Haemorrhoids.

CYNTHIA   Well I certainly wasn't informed about this!

PRATT   Well, it is rather a personal matter, madam.

CYNTHIA   No, I mean it could change everything. Really, Colonel, it's most remiss of you.

CHARLES   Sorry and all that. Didn't realise.

CYNTHIA   I'll have to have a rethink. Now, will you please go upstairs and prepare for this evening. You know what you need to do?

CHARLES   Oh, absolutely.

NURSE   I'll change your dressing upstairs then, Colonel.

CYNTHIA   Dressing?

PRATT   The Colonel has poultry applied to his grout.

               (CHARLES *and* NURSE *move towards the hall door.*)

CHARLES   Rightio. See you later then I suppose, Inspector.

               (PRATT *moves over to* CHARLES, *protectively.*)

PRATT I will escort you, Colonel. Your safety is now my responsibility. From this moment forward I am your bodyguard.

CHARLES Really, old boy, you're not going to follow me everywhere are you? Chap needs a bit of privacy . . . 'specially with his nurse.

(NURSE *giggles*.)

PRATT Have no fear, Colonel Haddock. I am fully trained in the arts of body guarding. I have mastered all the essential bodily functions. I will be like a shadow. You will not see me . . . you will not hear me . . . but I will always be present, lurking in the half light . . . stealthily stalking like a . . . a stealthily (*At a loss for words*.) . . . stalking . . . stalker.

(PRATT *draws his revolver from his coat and leaps into the hall. He glances around cautiously before beckoning the others.* CHARLES *and* NURSE *exit into the hall after him and they all disappear from view. Several seconds later a shot is heard from the hall followed by a scream from the nurse. There is absolute quiet, then* PRATT'S *voice is heard.*)

(*off*) Sorry.

(*There is silence again.* CYNTHIA *is thoughtful and moves to sit on the settee.* PUCHLIK *enters from the hall looking agitated and confused.*)

PUCHLIK Ah, Miss Maple. Who is crazy man with gun shooting at chandelier?

CYNTHIA If he's half the man my sister told me about I should imagine he missed.

PUCHLIK Is crazy people in this house.

(PUCHLIK *moves to the drinks table and pours himself a scotch.*)

Do you care for drink, Miss Maple?

(CYNTHIA *does not respond.* PUCHLIK *moves towards her. She finally glances up at him.*)

CYNTHIA   Sorry. You said?

PUCHLIK   I say do you want drink?

CYNTHIA   No . . . absolutely not.

PUCHLIK   Is very good . . . scotch whisky.

CYNTHIA   So I'm told. I never drink, Count Puchlik. In my business I need to keep my wits about me.

PUCHLIK   Is sometimes good to take drink. Sometimes is good to forget. Take my country, Poland. I fear that my people may soon have many things to forget.

CYNTHIA   In what respect, Count?

PUCHLIK   The storm clouds are gathering over my country. Soon we may have no country.

CYNTHIA   Oh, you mean Herr Hitler. I've no time for him. He's quite mad.

PUCHLIK   He is very dangerous but I do not believe that he is mad.

CYNTHIA   Don't agree. You only have to hear the man ranting and raving.

PUCHLIK   I have what you English call humorous impression of Herr Hitler. It amuses my friends very much. Do you wish me to show you?

CYNTHIA   (*standing and moving towards the hall door*) I really don't think so, Count. I have many things to do.

PUCHLIK   But will only take one moment. (*Replacing his glass on the sideboard and moving behind a chair which he uses like a lectern.*) My friends say is very amusing. I show you.

(*Throughout the following speech,* PUCHLIK *rants in a strong German accent.* CYNTHIA *watches in silence.*)

Achtung, achtung. Ve shall take over the ze entire vorld. No one vill be safe from ze great German Imperial var machine because ve have ze very large panzers.

(*He glances at* CYNTHIA *with a slightly embarrassed grin on his face, seeking approval. She smiles at him coldly.*)

You Englanders vill be placed against ze vall unt dealt vith very very nastily indeed.

(PUCHLIK *goose-steps around in front of the chairs.* CYNTHIA *watches him in amazement, shaking her head. When his back is turned she leaves the room quietly.*)

Zere vill be no escape. Ve shall take everyone from zis house unt interrogate zem. Ve shall make zem spill ze beans as you English say. For you ze var vill be over before it is even begun. (*Reverting to his normal accent.*) Is very amusing, yes?

(*He turns to where* CYNTHIA *was standing, pleased with his performance and is surprised to find that she has gone.*)

(*sadly*) Maybe is not so amusing.

(PUCHLIK *moves towards the hall door and then changes his mind. He walks to the secret panel, glancing over his shoulder furtively before stepping through into the passageway, shutting the secret panel behind him.* MARTHA *enters from the hall. She is dressed plainly as the housekeeper. She is followed by* HENRIETTA.)

MARTHA   (*as she enters*) He's in here, he's up to no good, you mark my words. (*Looking around she realises that the room is empty.*) Well he was in here. I heard him as clear as anything. He's one of those Nazi people. You want to shoot him or take him prisoner or something.

HENRIETTA   But I think that might be tricky. We're not actually at war with anybody at the moment. It's probably considered bad form to go around shooting people willy-nilly. Anyway we haven't any proof.

MARTHA   What more proof do you need? I'd just hung my coat up as I came back from the village and I heard him, ranting and raving like a lunatic. We're all going to be put against the wall, they're like that.

HENRIETTA   Gosh! Look, I'm sure you must be mistaken. Seemed like a decent enough fellow to me. He is Polish, he's got a bit of an accent, that's all.

MARTHA   But this was different.

HENRIETTA   Well, I'm sorry and all that . . . like to help, but no can do I'm afraid.

MARTHA   Well, if you won't listen, I'll just have to find someone who will.

HENRIETTA   (*sharply*) No . . . don't do that.

MARTHA   I'll have to. It's my duty.

HENRIETTA   Look, leave it with me and I'll do a spot of
              digging if you like. Maybe you're right. The
              Country needs more people like you, keeping
              their eyes and ears open.

MARTHA   I'm just doing my bit.

HENRIETTA   Absolutely. But for the time being, it's
              probably best to keep it our little secret.

MARTHA   (*reluctant*)All right then. But I'm right, as sure
              as eggs is eggs.

HENRIETTA   Well if he is a beastly old Hun, I'll find out,
              make no mistake.

MARTHA   I know people think I interfere but . . . anyway,
              I'm glad I've told someone. (*Glancing at the
              fireplace.*) Oh, look at that! All the logs gone.
              I'd best go and fetch some more. (*Picking up
              the log scuttle.*) It was starting to snow quite
              heavily as I came back from the village. Think
              we're in for quite a covering.

              (MARTHA *moves to exit into the hallway.*
              HENRIETTA *spots the nurses cape and picks it
              up, draping it around* MARTHA'S *shoulders.*)

HENRIETTA   Can't have you catching your death of cold.
              Not someone as valuable to the country as
              you.

MARTHA   Oh, but this is Nurse's!

HENRIETTA   I'm sure she won't mind if you borrow it.

MARTHA   Well, I suppose I won't be a minute. I always
              wanted to be a nurse.

              (MARTHA *exits into the hallway.* HENRIETTA
              *watches her go. She frowns, thinks for a
              moment, and then moves over to the secret*

panel and exits through it. PRATT *enters
dramatically from the hall. He is carrying his
revolver and checks the room for danger
before shouting out to* CHARLES *who is in the
hall.*)

PRATT

It is perfectly safe to enter, Colonel. No one is
within.

(CHARLES *enters, dressed formally for dinner.*)

CHARLES

I wish you wouldn't insist on carrying that
blasted thing around, old boy. I wouldn't mind
if you knew how to use the thing.

PRATT

Don't be deceived by my casual manner,
Colonel. The revolver is a sophisticated but
deadly weapon of distraction in the hand of a
fully trained expert.

(PRATT *attempts to spin the revolver in his
fingers but it spins away through the air.*
PRATT *panics and winces, putting his hands
over his ears.*)

CHARLES

(*in panic*) Steady on, man!

(*The revolver lands on the floor harmlessly.*)

PRATT

Just demonstrating a little trick I learnt, Colonel
. . . (*Thinking hard.*) the old tossing the gun
away ploy as we call it on the force. Whilst the
dangerous criminal is memorised by the tossing
of the gun, I would approach him rapidly and
dissemble him with a single blow . . .
(*Demonstrating a karate chop.*) . . . to the
sarcophagus. A cunning but effective
manoeuvre.

(PRATT *moves to the gun and prods it carefully
to make sure that is safe. He carefully picks it
up.*)

There are more ways than one to skin a bat,
Colonel Haddock.

(PRATT *aims the gun into the air. A dinner
gong sounds very loudly from off right. Pratt
examines his gun in surprise.* MARTHA *enters
from the hall, carrying the log scuttle which is
full of logs.*)

MARTHA   (*crossing to the fireplace*) There's the dinner
gong, Colonel, eight o'clock on the dot.

CHARLES   Rightio. Best get moving along then. Are you
coming through, Inspector?

PRATT   Allow me.

(PRATT *moves to the dining room door and
exits cautiously, waving his gun. He finally re-
enters, standing in the doorway.*)

Quite safe, Colonel. No one lies in wait without.
I will wait within until you are without in order
to cover your movement.

CHARLES   Whatever you like, old boy.

(*There is a scramble in the doorway as*
CHARLES *tries to get past* PRATT, *with them both
side-stepping several times, blocking each
other. Eventually* CHARLES *grabs hold of* PRATT
*and spins both of them through one hundred
and eighty degrees.* CHARLES *exits.* PRATT *tries
to follow him but the door is firmly shut in his
face. He glances back towards* MARTHA *and,
seeing her watching him, casually pretends
that he is inspecting the door frame for
imperfections.* MARTHA *is using a brush to
sweep the hearth.*)

MARTHA   I don't expect this weather's going to get any
better tonight, sir. I think we'll be snowed in
before too long.

PRATT

I think not. It takes more than a few drops of snow to disable a Pratt like me.

(CARDEW *enters from the hall. He is dressed exactly the same as* CHARLES. MARTHA *finishes sweeping and backs away towards the secret panel. She finishes with her back pressed against the secret panel, watching the following events.*)

CARDEW

Good evening, good sir. We are summoned to an event of a gastronomic nature I believe.

(PRATT *looks at* CARDEW *in amazement. He has several double takes between* CARDEW *and the dining room.*)

PRATT

(*pointing in amazement into the dining room*) You just went in there!

CARDEW

I fear you are wrong, sir. (*Pointing to the hall door.*) I have but moments ago entered here and now seek egress through yonder portal. If you would permit me passage, dear fellow.

(*There is an identical scramble to the previous one as* CARDEW *tries to get past* PRATT *into the dining room. As the audience is partially distracted by the commotion stage right, the secret panel opens stage left and an unidentifiable hand drags* MARTHA *back into the secret passageway. The secret panel closes as* CARDEW *finally exits into the dining room.*)

PRATT

(*gazing off into the dining room*) Did you see that? (*Slapping his own face.*) I've never seen anything like it. Unbelievable.

(PRATT *backs towards the hall doorway and peers through it, still unable to believe what he's seen. As he looks out, the secret panel opens again and* MARTHA *stumbles out and stands awkwardly, supporting herself against the chair back. A large pair of scissors can be seen protruding from the top of her back. She stands rigid, glassy eyed as the panel shuts behind her. PRATT moves back into the room.)*

I'm a police officer . . . very little gets past my finely honed defective brain but I don't know how he managed to move that fast!

MARTHA   (*gasping*) Need help.

PRATT   (*moving up to* MARTHA) I expect he would. Good thinking. Some sort of trolley arrangement if I'm not mistaken . . . lots of pulleys. Well done. Well done, Missus Armpit.

                (PRATT *turns to exit into the dining room. As he moves away from her she slumps to the floor. PRATT exits as the lights fade and the curtain falls.*)

Scene Two

Later the same evening. They are all assembled in the library with the exception of CARDEW. ISADORA and CYNTHIA are seated on the settee and NURSE PARSLEY is seated on the more central of the two chairs. CHARLES stands behind her with LILY close by. PUCHLIK and HENRIETTA stand behind the settee. PRATT paces in exasperation, centre stage.

PRATT   This is a very serious business. Very, very serious indeed.

PUCHLIK   Is very sad. Such nice lady is dead. My eyes weep for her.

PRATT   (*gravely*) But *how* is she dead? That's what I want to know. That is the one and only question which faces us.

CYNTHIA   And *why* is she dead?

PRATT	Exactly . . . exactly. That's the other question.
PUCHLIK	Excuse, but you said there was only one question.
PRATT	Very well. Those are the two questions . . . all right?
CHARLES	I would have thought *when* was pretty important too, old boy.
PRATT	Very good, Colonel. How, why and when.
PUCHLIK	This is now three questions, Inspector.
PRATT	(*losing patience*) Who's counting. It's not important. I was speaking figuratively.
PUCHLIK	But you were using wrong figures, Inspector.
PRATT	All right . . . all right. If you want to be a pendant. I was speaking . . . metamorphically . . . will that do you?
PUCHLIK	I believe you are meaning metaphorically, Inspector.
PRATT	I know what I mean! Foreign, aren't you?
PUCHLIK	I am.
PRATT	Well, just watch your step then.
PUCHLIK	(*waving his dictionary*) Metaphor is phrase applied to an object in order to imply a resemblance.
PRATT	Quite. Proves my point exactly. I said *one question* where I was actually implying *three questions*. Does that clear it up for you, eh? QED as they say in France.

CYNTHIA   I think you'll find it's Latin, Inspector.

PRATT   What?

CYNTHIA   Latin.

PRATT   Obviously, yes. That's what I meant. The Latin
               quarter in Paris. They say it with monotonous
               regularity. QED . . . Quad . . . (*Struggling*.) . . .
               eroticus . . . delecto . . . as they say. Is
               everybody assembled, Colonel?

CHARLES   (*glancing around the room*) All except that
               Longfellow chap.

PRATT   And the housekeeper if I'm not mistaken.

CHARLES   She's the one who's dead, old boy.

PRATT   Is she? Is she indeed? Quite right, Colonel.
               That would explain her abstinence. This
               Longfellow fellow . . . where is he?

CYNTHIA   He's not feeling well, Inspector. He found the
               body if you remember.

PRATT   I remember very well indeed. And I must ask
               why you are trying to deceive me, Miss
               Maypole. As I recall, it was Colonel Haddock
               who found the unfortunate deceased. Am I not
               correct, Colonel?

CHARLES   No, old boy. It was Longfellow. He's the chap
               who looks like me.

PRATT   (*suspicious*) Mmm. (*Moving towards*
               HENRIETTA.) Nurse Partridge . . .

               (HENRIETTA *shakes her head and points
               towards* NURSE. PRATT *changes direction and
               moves towards* NURSE.)

Nurse Partridge, you had the opportunity to
examine the dead deceased person?

NURSE   Yes, I examined the corpse. But I'm not really
             trained in post-mortem examination.

PRATT   Of course not. But what about dead people?
             How long had she been in a corpulent
             condition.

NURSE   (*helpfully, but completely out of her depth and
             not with any conviction*) Well, I think she'd
             probably been dead for over an hour when she
             was found. She seemed quite stiff.

PRATT   (*impressed with the* NURSE'S *analysis*) Thank
             you, Nurse Partridge. Now, the thing we have
             to do is establish all of your whereabouts. By
             whereabouts, I mean, where abouts were you.
             Do any of you have an alibi? (*He pronounces it
             aleebee.*) Now, let us examine the facts.
             (*Pulling a note book from his pocket.*) Fact
             number one. Missus Martha Housekeeper is
             dead. (*He scans several more pages of his
             notebook quickly and then replaces it
             uncertainly in his pocket.*)

CYNTHIA   Is that it?

PRATT   Are you telling us that you know more, Miss
             Maypole?

CYNTHIA   Of course I do.

PRATT   (*laughing*) So, you have fallen into my
             cunningly contrived trap. Only the murderer
             would know more.

ISADORA   Excuse me, Inspector, but I believe that we all
             know a little more.

PRATT   Now we're making progress. (*Backing away
                 nervously towards the hall door.*) You mean
                 you're all in it together?

ISADORA   Hardly, Inspector. The fact is that when Mister
                 Longfellow found her, we had all been seated
                 at dinner together for the previous hour and a
                 quarter. No one left the room until Mister
                 Longfellow found her.

PRATT   So?

ISADORA   So, unless someone killed her immediately
                 before coming into dinner, it can't have been
                 any of us.

HENRIETTA   Gosh, yes. You're absolutely right. Jolly clever.

PRATT   Very good, Lady Pollock. You're catching on.
                 But of course, this new evidence opens up a
                 very interesting question. Who was the last
                 person to see Missus Housekeeper alive? If we
                 find the answer to that, we have our murderer.
                 The last person to see her alive must have been
                 the first person to see her dead.

CHARLES   (*moving to* PRATT) Must have been you, old
                 boy. When Longfellow came through to the
                 dining room, he said you were talking to her in
                 here.

PRATT   Very clever, Colonel, but that doesn't nessa . . .
                 celery make me the last person to see her.

LILY   I think it does, sir.

PRATT   What?

LILY   I was waiting to serve up, but I couldn't 'til
                 you'd all seated yourselves. You were the last
                 to come into the dining room.

PRATT   Ah!

CHARLES   So you're the murderer, old boy. Must be.

PRATT   Don't be ridiculous, Colonel. I'm a police
                 officer of the law. I detect crime, not commit it.

CYNTHIA   You don't seem to have detected too much so
                 far. Never seen anything like it. My sister was
                 right about you.

PRATT   (*moving to* CYNTHIA) And what did your sister
                 say about me?

CYNTHIA   Well, if you really must know, she thought you
                 were a nincompoop.

PRATT   A noncimpoop, eh? Well, would a nicpomnoop
                 have an answer to our little mystery as I have
                 got?

                 (*They all remain silent.*)

                 That surprises you? (*Backing away from*
                 CYNTHIA *and turning at the last moment
                 finding himself face to face with* CHARLES.) Yes
                 indeed, having examined all the facts at my
                 dispersal, I now have the solution to our
                 condominium. We need look no further.

HENRIETTA   You mean you've solved it already? That's
                 terribly clever.

PRATT   Ah yes. To all of you, this may seem like an
                 impossible task. A series of unconnected
                 rancid events which have no meaning, which
                 lead nowhere. To me, it's a jigsaw, where every
                 piece has a place . . . a game of chess where
                 you are the prawns and I am the Queen bee.

ISADORA   So, who was it, Inspector?

PRATT   Is it not obvious to any of you? Am I the only
                 light in an otherwise unlightened dark place of
                 gloomy ignorance?

ISADORA   (*glancing around the room*) It would seem so,
                 Inspector.

PRATT   Very well, I will attempt to elucidate your
                 glumness. I was the last person to see Missus
                 Housemartin. We all met for dinner.
                 Immediately on completion of dinner, her body
                 was found. She had been corpulating for some
                 time. We need look no further. There is no
                 murderer . . . but we do have that age old killer
                 . . . Mister Coronary (*He pronounce it cor-own-
                 ary.*) Thombostic.

                 (*They all look at him in confused silence.*)

                 Yes . . . so obvious. In fact, so obvious that
                 none of you were able to see through the fog
                 of obviousness except me. You may all leave.
                 You are free to go.

CHARLES   I think you may be missing something, old boy.

PRATT   I think not, Colonel.

CHARLES   Well, look, old boy . . . I'm not a medical man, I
                 admit that.

PRATT   Then perhaps you should stick to what you
                 know best, Colonel.

CHARLES   It's just that I rather thought there may be
                 another factor in the equation.

PRATT   I see. (*Smiling smugly at the others.*) Then I'm
                 sure that we are all anxious to hear your
                 equation.

(As CHARLES *makes the following speech,* PRATT *is so busy smiling nonchalantly at the others that his words barely register.)*

CHARLES   Well, as I said, I'm not a medical man, but I'd rather assumed that the enormous pair of scissors which were sticking out of her back might have had something to do with the cause of death.

PRATT   An easy mistake to make, Colonel, an easy . . . (CHARLES'S *words finally sink in.*) . . . scissors! What scissors! (*Examining his notebook.*)

NURSE   The scissors I gave to you, Inspector, after I'd examined her.

CYNTHIA   The rather large scissors, Inspector.

PUCHLIK   Which were embedded six inches into the lady's back.

PRATT   Ah, those scissors. (*Thinking quickly.*) I hadn't forgotten them of course. In my estimation they were a secondary cause of death . . . causing death shortly after the initial death.

ISADORA   Forgive me, Inspector but I don't quite understand.

PRATT   Of course you don't. But we are trained to piece together a visual picture of events. (*Miming the events as he describes them.*) I believe that Missus Housemartin was using the scissors for some kind of scissoring activity. At the moment of heart seizure, she inadvertently hurled the scissors into the air as she clasped her hands to her bosom. Now, as she fell forward, the scissors would come tumbling back to earth, embedding themselves in her back, Though, of course, by this time she was already corpulent. A classic case of post-mortal death.

(CHARLES *wearies of the nonsense and moves to the sideboard to pour himself a drink.*)

CYNTHIA   You really don't have the faintest idea do you, Inspector?

PRATT   You have a better theory?

CYNTHIA   It's quite obvious that the woman was killed by some intruder who is probably now long gone. A sneak thief who was trying to take advantage of the fact that we were all at dinner. He could have seen us clearly in the light of the dining room from outside . . . (*Self recriminating.*) Oh, if only one of us had drawn the curtains!

ISADORA   I do think you could be right there, Miss Maple. Yes, of course. It's so obvious.

HENRIETTA   Bravo, Miss Maple. Well done.

ISADORA   You must agree, Inspector that it seems quite obvious.

PRATT   (*sulking*) Not necessarily.

PUCHLIK   But more likely than your explanation, Inspector.

PRATT   Not at all. Mine was far better. I certainly don't see how a sketch of the curtains would have saved Miss Household.

CYNTHIA   (*wearily*) I said draw . . . not sketch.

PRATT   Don't try to confuse the issue with semitics, Miss Mayfly. (*Indicating* PUCHLIK.) You're getting as bad as him! Anyway, I'm in charge and it's my explanation that counts.

CYNTHIA	Nonsense. It's quite clear, Inspector that you'd be far better continuing your investigations down in the village amongst known criminals.
PRATT	I see. Why do you wish to see me depart so suddenly? Do you have something to hide?
CYNTHIA	Don't be so ridiculous.
PRATT	I shall leave when I wish to leave and not before . . . or after for that matter. As it happens I may decide that I wish to leave now.
CHARLES	I don't think you'll be going anywhere tonight, old boy. Have you had a look outside lately? Bit of a blizzard. You'll never get the car out.
PRATT	(*moving to* CHARLES) No matter, Colonel. I have my golloshers in the boot.
CHARLES	You're not thinking of walking?
PRATT	Not walking, Colonel. Running.
CHARLES	In golloshers! You'll never make it.
PRATT	I am an experienced cross-country runner, Colonel. I have often been compared with a goat.
CYNTHIA	I'll bet you have.
PRATT	Nothing can stop me. The abominable Pratt as I'm known on the force.
CHARLES	Suit yourself, old boy. It's just that several people have died around here in these conditions. Still, if you're quite sure.
PRATT	Died!
LILY	He's right, sir.

CHARLES	No landmarks, do you see? People get lost in the whiteout and wander off into the hills . . .
LILY	And die 'orrible deaths.
CHARLES	Chap who killed poor Martha is probably out there himself . . . lost . . . wandering . . . desperate.
LILY	Desperate for food I would think. Probably so desperate he'd eat anything . . . even another desperate wanderer.
CHARLES	Still, Inspector, no point dwelling on the matter. I'll get your coat if you insist.
PRATT	On second thoughts, Colonel, I may prevail on your hospitality until meatylogical conditions improve. No point me rushing away into the night leaving you all unprotected.
CHARLES	Very wise, old boy.
CYNTHIA	If you're staying perhaps you might like to pit your wits against the other guests, Inspector?
PRATT	Pit my wits?
CYNTHIA	We have a little mystery planned for later this evening.
CHARLES	You're not still carrying on with that nonsense are you! Dash it all, poor woman's been killed here tonight.
CYNTHIA	Not by any of us. No point moping about the place. It might take our minds off the matter.
ISADORA	Perhaps she's right, Colonel. It may help to pass the time . . . create a little diversion.

CHARLES Seems dashed bad form to me. Bad business . . . the whole thing. I mean she was a dashed good housekeeper, where am I going to find another one like that? Tragic. Still, if you insist. You're the guests.

CYNTHIA Then I suggest we all reconvene in here in twenty minutes and we will commence. Just time for the ladies to freshen up.

ISADORA What an admirable idea.

(ISADORA *and* NURSE *stand, move towards the hall door and exit.* LILY *moves towards the dining room door.*)

LILY I'll 'ave to wash up, never mind this freshen up lark.

(LILY *exits.* CYNTHIA *stands and moves towards the hall door.*)

PRATT Perhaps I might use your telephone, Colonel Herring, to report my excellent progress on the case.

CHARLES Course you can, old boy. I'll take you to my study.

PRATT What for?

CHARLES To use the phone.

PRATT Ah yes, the phone . . . that'll be in the study.

CYNTHIA (*by the hall door as she exits*) Twenty minutes on the dot, Colonel.

CHARLES Absolutely, old girl. This way, old boy.

(CHARLES *leads* PRATT *off through the dining room.* HENRIETTA *and* PUCHLIK *are left in the room.* PUCHLIK *moves towards the dining room door and checks to make sure that no one is listening. Satisfied, he closes the door and turns back to* HENRIETTA.)

PUCHLIK The storm clouds are gathering over Europe, Captain.

HENRIETTA (*moving down*) Rather think we've been through all that.

PUCHLIK (*insistent*) The storm clouds are gathering over Europe.

HENRIETTA (*sighing*) I haven't had the chance to see the full forecast myself.

PUCHLIK (*reverting to his strong German accent, standing to attention, clicking his heels together and giving the Nazi salute*) Heinrich Kuchler at your service. It is important that we use ze secret identification phrases at all times.

HENRIETTA (*in an urgent serious voice, quite unlike her normal voice*) It's hardly necessary. We have met before!

PUCHLIK (*moving to* HENRIETTA) Security is vital to my mission. The future of the third Reich rests on my shoulders.

HENRIETTA Look we haven't got long. You'll have to come to my room, I have some urgent messages for you.

PUCHLIK Ah, ze secret messages from ze glorious Fuhrer himself. I think things are progressing very satisfactorily, ja?

HENRIETTA I'm really not bothered how things progress! When do I get the money for all of this.

PUCHLIK   Soon my pretty little friend, soon. How easily
                 your British comrades are fooled. My little
                 invention, Count Puchlik, is rapidly becoming
                 accepted amongst your aristocracy. When ze
                 time comes he will be vell placed to learn all
                 their little vartime secrets.

HENRIETTA   And if you want me to help you transmit these
                 little 'vartime' secrets that will cost you more.
                 Understood?

PUCHLIK   Always you talk about money. I do all of this
                 for ze glory of ze Fatherland.

HENRIETTA   Well, I don't give a damn about glory . . . but I
                 do care a lot about money, I have very
                 expensive tastes.

PUCHLIK   (*during* PUCHLIK'S *following two speeches, his
                 voice becomes increasingly loud and excited*)
                 Just think, my friend, soon it vill all begin. Ze
                 panzers vill strike the Polish swine. Then we
                 vill roll across France and finally grind you
                 Britishers into ze ground like so many
                 insignificant ants.

HENRIETTA   Don't forget about the English channel. I'd
                 hate you to get your feet wet.

PUCHLIK   That puny stretch of water! That vill not stop
                 our panzers. Not after our magnificent Bismarck
                 has sunk your jolly jack tars. Zen I, Heinrich
                 Kuchler vill be at ze Fuhrer's right hand as he
                 steps into Buckingham Palace to demand ze
                 surrender of your king. Then ze king vill be
                 shot.

                 (PUCHLIK *becomes increasingly excited and his
                 voice rises to a crescendo.* HENRIETTA *gestures
                 for him to be quiet but this only enflames him
                 to a higher fever pitch.* HENRIETTA *quickly
                 checks that all seems quiet outside the hall
                 and dining room doors.*)

Resistance vill be futile. For all of you
Britishers the var will be over. You vill all be
shot and our glorious panzers vill conquer ze
whole world.

HENRIETTA   (*moving back to* PUCHLIK) Quiet! You'll be
heard!

PUCHLIK   (*sheepishly*) Sorry, my friend. I get over
excited. Alvays I have vanted to drive ze
panzers but my eye sight is not so good.

HENRIETTA   You've already been overheard once!

PUCHLIK   But zat was just my little joke. I know how
much ze stupid Britishers love ze joke of ze
foreigner with ze silly accent.

HENRIETTA   We're not here for jokes. The housekeeper took
it seriously. The last thing you need is
someone delving into the background of Count
Puchlik. They might get some nasty shocks.

PUCHLIK   (*laughing*) Like ze housekeeper received ze
shock, ja?

HENRIETTA   (*smiling*) *She* certainly won't cause us anymore
trouble, that's for sure.

(PRATT'S *voice is heard off, in the dining room.*)

PRATT   (*off*) Colonel . . . Colonel Kipper?

HENRIETTA   Come on, quickly, up to my room.

(HENRIETTA *and* PUCHLIK *exit into the hall.*
PRATT *enters from the dining room seconds
later.*)

PRATT   Colonel Kipper? . . . (*Looking around and
moving behind the settee.*) Ah, as I thought, an
empty room.

LILY

(*off, in the dining room*) Inspector? Could I 'ave a word. (*Entering from the dining room.*) There you are, Inspector, I've been chasing you 'alf way round the 'ouse.

PRATT

Yes, here I am indeed Missus Tuthill. Here I am alone . . . in this empty room . . . except for you of course.

LILY

I was 'oping to 'ave a word in a more private part of the 'ouse. I suppose 'ere'll do.

PRATT

Indeed. That is one thing that never ceases to amaze me in my job, Missus Tuthill . . . (*Bored he turns and moves to examine books on the bookcase, stage left.*) . . . everyone wants to see me in their private parts.

LILY

(*in a serious, forceful and educated voice, quite unlike her normal accent*) There are things that you need to know, Inspector.

(PRATT *is taken by surprise by the different voice. He spins on his heels, looking suspiciously round the room.*)

PRATT

Have a care, Missus Tuthill. I hear a strange voice. I suspect that we are not alone.

(LILY *watches in surprise as* PRATT *moves cautiously to the hall door, adopting the stance of an incompetent karate fighter.* LILY *in turn checks that no one is in the dining room.*)

LILY

(*confused, in her broad accent*) Why, whatever gives you that idea, Inspector? I didn't 'ear anything.

PRATT

Perhaps not, but I have the all-seeing ears of a hawk.

(PRATT *raises his hand, indicating that she should remain silent. He suddenly jerks open the hall door and leaps into the hall, disappearing from view with a banshee scream.*)

(*finally, off*) As I suspected . . . no one.

LILY   (*moving past the hall door, towards the stage left bookcase and adopting her serious voice*) Then we must talk, Inspector. We probably won't have much time.

PRATT   (*off, in alarm*) There it is again. Hold fast, Missus Anthill.

(PRATT *suddenly leaps back into the room with his gun in his hand. He performs an inadequate somersault, finishing behind the settee. He tries to prop his elbows on the settee, gun in hand, but immediately slips down again out of sight.*)

LILY   (*suddenly, in her businesslike voice*) Whatever are you doing, Inspector?

(PRATT *leaps to his feet with a terrified squeal.*)

PRATT   (*seeing* LILY) It's you!

LILY   Of course it's me.

PRATT   (*suspiciously*) What have you done with her?

LILY   With who?

PRATT   Missus Anthill.

LILY   Tuthill.

PRATT   That's what I said. Foothill.

LILY   Well obviously, I'm her.

PRATT   (*even more suspicious*) Then what have you done with her voice? There are two Colonel Kipper's . . . are there two of you?

LILY   No of course not, there's only one of me. (*moving to him*) Now listen, we haven't much time.

PRATT   Why are you talking like that?

LILY   Because I'm not really Lily Tuthill.

PRATT   You just said you were.

LILY   (*exasperated*) I'm only pretending to be Lily Tuthill, the cook. It's my cover. It's an alias. I work for British Intelligence. I'm on a highly secret mission.

PRATT   Doing what?

LILY   I can't tell you that, it's highly secret.

PRATT   I see.

LILY   Listen, Inspector, I can't afford for you to make a mess of everything by blundering about. I don't know why Martha was killed. It may not be connected with my mission but we have to be very careful how we move.

PRATT   Do we? Yes we do.

LILY   I hope I can rely on you, Inspector.

PRATT   Of course. We're all on the same side aren't we?

LILY	I certainly hope so. Look, you stay here and keep your eye open for anything suspicious. I have other things to take care of.
PRATT	Very good.

(PRATT *tiptoes cautiously away from* LILY, *ending with his back to the upstage bookcase.*)

LILY	What are you doing, Inspector?
PRATT	You said we had to move cautiously.
LILY	Oh, my God!

(LILY *exits to the dining room, shaking her head.* PRATT *watches her go, glances around the room, uncertain what to do, then cautiously tiptoes off after her. The lights fade, indicating a short passage of time.*)

(*When the lights rise,* PRATT *is sprawled asleep on the settee and* HENRIETTA *is seated next to him jotting notes into a notebook.* PUCHLIK *is seated on the stage left chair reading a book.* CYNTHIA *enters carrying some notes, followed by* ISADORA *who is dressed rather tartily.*)

CYNTHIA	Are we all ready?
PUCHLIK	We have been waiting for some time.
ISADORA	Oh, I'm terribly sorry, Count Puchlik. It's entirely my fault. I wanted to make sure that I really looked my part. This is all so exciting.
CYNTHIA	Might I have your attention then if you don't mind.

(PUCHLIK *puts his book to one side and*
HENRIETTA *places her notebook in a pocket.*
PRATT *still sleeps.*)

HENRIETTA   I didn't realise we had to dress up already?

CYNTHIA   In your case there is no need at the moment.
You will make your entrance later but it is
important that you observe the first part of our
little pastiche. Now . . . (*Referring to her
notes.*) . . . are you all listening carefully?

(*They all nod.*)

Very good. Let me explain the current
situation . . .

(PRATT *suddenly snores very violently and
settles back contentedly into the armchair.*)

Who was that!

(*They all point accusingly at* PRATT.)

I see.

(CYNTHIA *moves behind* PRATT'S *chair and talks
firmly to him.*)

Wake up, Inspector.

(PRATT *snores again.* CYNTHIA *shouts, shaking
his shoulder.*)

Wake up!

(PRATT *keeps his eyes shut and mutters.*)

PRATT   Not tonight, dear, have a cup of cocoa instead.

CYNTHIA   (*shouting louder*) Inspector!

(PRATT *opens one eye and stares around. He slowly becomes aware of his surroundings. He suddenly leaps smartly to his feet and immediately becomes very officious.*)

PRATT	So, has anyone anything more to add?
ISADORA	To what, Inspector?
PRATT	(*confused*) To whatever it was that we were talking about. About the investigation.
ISADORA	We weren't talking about an investigation.
CYNTHIA	You fell asleep!
PRATT	Asleep! Don't underestimate me, madam. I never fall asleep on the job. I was simply resting my frontal cranial lobotomy area after a hard day's detection.
CYNTHIA	You weren't on any job. We were about to start our pastiche.
PRATT	(*patting his stomach appreciatively and sitting down again*) Not for me, I couldn't eat another thing.
CYNTHIA	Pastiche . . . our little composition of various scenes.
PRATT	Ah yes, the re-enactment. I hadn't forgotten. That little charade was simply an impromptu finale to what is about to happen.
CYNTHIA	Fascinating. (*Referring to her notes.*) We are in the sitting room of a mansion. Lady Isadora is Charlotte, an American lady of poor reputation.
PRATT	Is she really? (*Reaching in his pocket for his notebook.*) I don't believe I have that recorded.

CYNTHIA	(*impatient*) She is a fictitious character . . . Charlotte. She doesn't really exist.
PRATT	Doesn't she indeed? That sounds even more suspicious. (*Writing in his notebook.*) Lady Isadora is a shallot.
CYNTHIA	(*increasingly frustrated*) Charlotte! She's fictitious!
PRATT	Don't try to confuse me, Miss Mayday. I can see her. I know my onions.
ISADORA	(*helpfully*) I think you're missing the point, Inspector. This is just a little drama in which we all play a small cameo role. I am to play the part of Charlotte. You, I believe, are to play the part of the butler.
PRATT	Am I? Oh, I see. (*Warming to the idea that he is included.*) I have a part?
CYNTHIA	Yes, Inspector. Unfortunately you have. You are to play the role of Smythes, the butler. A very small part I'm pleased to say. I suggest you stand by the sideboard, as befits your position as butler. Count Puchlik is a member of parliament, whom Charlotte is about to seduce.
PRATT	Is she indeed?
	(PRATT *moves to take up position by the sideboard. As he passes* PUCHLIK *he touches his nose and nods and winks knowingly.*)
CYNTHIA	So if you are all ready . . . begin.
	(*During the following sequence* PRATT *watches events unfold with increasing fascination, smiling happily, completely lost in the make-believe.*)

ISADORA   (*pulling a note of her character from her
             handbag*) Should I start?

CYNTHIA   If you wish. Unless someone starts very soon
             we'll all have fallen asleep again.

ISADORA   Very well. (*Taking an anxious glance at her
             notes and concentrating hard, she affects what
             she believes is a coarse American accent.*)
             What a crazy little house this is. Have yer been
             here long yourself?

PUCHLIK   (*hand effeminately on hip, trying very hard at
             an upper class English accent, preceding
             vowels with the letter 'h'*) Actually, I have
             arrived only some short time ago. Would you
             care to take tea with me.

ISADORA   I'd rather have something stronger if yer know
             what I mean. How 'bout you?

             (ISADORA *moves seductively over to* PUCHLIK
             and stands behind him stroking his head.)

PUCHLIK   Steady on now. What if Charles should arrive
             unexpectedly. What would he say?

ISADORA   Who gives a damn! (*Clicking her fingers at*
             PRATT.) Gimme a cigar for the gentleman.

PUCHLIK   I don't smoke, madam.

ISADORA   By the time I've finished with yer you'll be
             smoking fifty a day! (*Realising that* PRATT *is
             simply watching, fascinated.*) Hey, come on.
             We ain't got all day!

CYNTHIA   Inspector. You're the butler.

PRATT   Right. I've never butled before. It's very good,
             isn't it?

CYNTHIA   You are supposed to be part of it.

PRATT   I know, I know. What am I supposed to be
              doing?

ISADORA   Never mind. Forget the cigar. Just stand back
              and watch the flames.

              (ISADORA *starts to stroke* PUCHLIK'S *hair and
              pouts at him seductively.*)

CYNTHIA   That's very good. (*Disapproving.*) In fact,
              rather too good.

              (CYNTHIA *moves hastily to the hall door and
              taps on it.*)

              (*shouting through the door*) Cue for jealous
              husband. Jealous husband, you should be on
              now.

              (CARDEW *enters from the dining room, dressed
              as* CHARLES *in a sports jacket, white shirt and
              tie. He wears a deer stalker hat with the flaps
              dangling down the side of his face. He sees*
              ISADORA *and* PUCHLIK.)

CARDEW   (*impersonating* CHARLES) Good God . . . what's
              all this!

ISADORA   (*backing away slightly from* PUCHLIK) Why,
              it's you, my dear. It's not what you think.

CARDEW   It's better not be, old girl. What the devil's
              going on?

PRATT   I think I can explain, Colonel. They're just
              acting.

CYNTHIA   He knows that.

PRATT   Does he?

CYNTHIA	He's acting as well. That's Mister Longfellow.
PRATT	Is it?
CYNTHIA	Of course it is. That's why he's here.
PRATT	He's very good.
CARDEW	Well, come on. I want an explanation. Chap returns home from shooting and finds all this sort of business going on. If you're not careful I'll be taking me twelve bore to the pair of you. What do you think to that?
PUCHLIK	It was not my fault. I was simply sitting here when Charlotte suddenly went wild.
CARDEW	Did she? Never heard anything like it.
ISADORA	Don't worry, darling. Here, have a drink and I'll explain the whole thing. (*Clicking her fingers at* PRATT.) Give him a stiff one.
PRATT	What?
ISADORA	I said give him a stiff one.
	(PRATT *looks totally bemused.*)
CYNTHIA	A drink, Smythes.
ISADORA	Scotch on the rocks.
PRATT	(*trying to join in, he attempts an accent which comes out more like a west country farmer*) Ooh ar me lady, a scotch be coming right up.
	(*During the following speeches,* PRATT *pours a whisky into a glass.*)
ISADORA	(*moving to* CARDEW *and winding herself around him*) A little drink'll make yer feel real

good, honey. Then we can all sit down and talk about this little ol' mistake.

CARDEW
Really! Never seen anything like it. Chap never knows where he stands these days. Dashed bad form and all that sort of thing.

(PRATT *moves towards* CARDEW *with the drink in his hand. As he walks he places one hand over the top of the glass and shakes it exuberantly like a cocktail shaker. Finally he stops.*)

PRATT
Here are be your drink, sir. I'll just be giving it one more shake.

(PRATT *starts to shake the drink again.* CYNTHIA *impatiently grabs the drink from him and passes it to* CARDEW.)

CYNTHIA
Just get on with it!

CARDEW
Ah, don't mind if I do. Down the hatch and all that.

(CARDEW *gulps down the drink in one go.*)

Right, old girl. About this business with the feller there. Time we got to the bottom of it.

ISADORA
Well, honey, there really ain't nothing to explain.

CARDEW
Jolly well is. I mean to say . . . (*Suddenly starting to slur his words as though slightly drunk.*) thought you were jolly well my young . . . young filly. Very hot in here. (*Pushing up his jacket sleeves and taking off his deer stalker, holding it in his left hand.*) Not at all sure I feel so well.

ISADORA   (*taking the glass out of* CARDEW'S *hand*)
                 You're drunk!

CARDEW   (*slurring even more*) I certainly am not.

                 (CARDEW *suddenly grabs his throat, coughing
                 and gasping. He staggers.*)

ISADORA   Why, honey, what's wrong?

                 (CARDEW *staggers around behind the settee
                 theatrically with the others watching. He
                 finally falls behind the settee. The others
                 applaud his performance loudly, stopping
                 momentarily as he places both hands on the
                 back of the settee, still clutching the deer
                 stalker in his left hand, and heaves his head
                 into view of the audience over the top of the
                 settee. He gasps and splutters before sinking
                 out of view. Again the others applaud,
                 stopping briefly as the hands appear over the
                 settee again before sinking out of view. His
                 left hand remains in sight, sliding to the left of
                 the settee and onto the floor, projecting out
                 towards centre stage from behind the base of
                 settee, still clutching the deer stalker. All the
                 audience must see is a shirt-sleeved arm and
                 hand clutching a deer stalker. In actual fact,
                 the hand that they see is that of a stand in,
                 dressed as* CARDEW, *who has entered through
                 the concealed hatch and been crouching
                 behind the settee in readiness. The actor who
                 plays* CARDEW *must then exit unseen through
                 the concealed hatch in preparation for his
                 forthcoming entrance as* CHARLES. *As the hand
                 finally comes to rest, the others give a round
                 of applause They all resume their normal
                 voices.*)

CYNTHIA   Well done, Mister Longfellow. An excellent
                 performance.

ISADORA   It really was tremendously good. I haven't seen anything quite like that since I was last in the West End. What next, Miss Maple?

CYNTHIA   After a short pause we shall move on to a little scene which takes place one hour later. You may arise now, Mister Longfellow.

(*The "stand in* CARDEW" *does not move.* CHARLES *enters from the hall.*)

CHARLES   Ready for me yet? Anyone care for a snifter?

CYNTHIA   We shall be recommencing shortly. (*Concerned, to* ISADORA.) Perhaps you'd help Mister Longfellow to his feet, he seems to have taken rather a bad fall.

(*During the following speech,* ISADORA *crouches down by the body.*)

CHARLES   Has he indeed. Did I ever tell you about the bad fall I had when I was hunting gazelle on horseback in Africa? I was on horseback of course, not the gazelle!

ISADORA   Colonel, I think I need your help.

CHARLES   Ah, yes, of course. Come along, old fellow. (*To* ISADORA.) Out of the way m'dear . . . let the chap have a spot of air.

(ISADORA *moves away as* CHARLES *crouches next to the body. As he looks at the body his expression turns to one of concern. He feels for a pulse at the wrist.*)

Ah. This could be dashed awkward!

CYNTHIA   Is there a problem, Colonel?

CHARLES   Not much I can do here. Chap's dead!

CYNTHIA   No, he's pretending to be dead . . . he's an
           actor.

CHARLES   Well he's a damn good one then. Chap's
           managed to stop his own pulse!

           (ISADORA *screams.* PRATT, *believing this to be*
           still a part of the pastiche, grins broadly and
           applauds loudly as the curtain falls.)

ACT TWO

Scene One

Several minutes later. The 'body' is now laid out on the settee and is covered by a sheet. It is actually the NURSE *who lies underneath the sheet.* CARDEW'S *shoes protrude from one end of the sheet, adding to the illusion that it is his body. His deer stalker lies on the arm of the settee.* CYNTHIA *and* ISADORA *are in the room.* CYNTHIA *paces up and down, agitated, while* ISADORA *sits quietly on one of the chairs, thinking.* PRATT *enters from the hall, preoccupied. He notices* CYNTHIA *and* ISADORA.

PRATT   Ah, ladies, if I may call you that.

CYNTHIA   Inspector.

PRATT   May I ask what you are doing in here? I gave
                 definite instructions that nobody was to
                 inhabitate this room until I had completed a
                 thorough pains-aching search.

CYNTHIA   What are you possibly going to find,
                 Inspector?

PRATT   Evidence of an irrefutable incriminating nature.
                 Perhaps even something that may help me
                 solve the case.

CYNTHIA   But he died of a heart attack. It's quite obvious
                 to anyone who has the slightest hint of a brain.

PRATT   But I don't have the slightest hint of a brain,
                 Missus Mayday. A heart attack! He was
                 poisoned! With a poisonous sustenance from
                 that very discounter over there!

CYNTHIA	That was only in the little play act we were performing. He was to pretend that he had been poisoned. It was in the script.
PRATT	Ah, but criminals don't always read the script . . . and the world is a bigger stage than you can shake a stick at.
	(They all look bemused by the last statement, even PRATT himself.)
ISADORA	It's a tragic coincidence, Inspector. Nothing more than that.
CYNTHIA	A very inconvenient coincidence if you ask me. Ruined the whole plot.
ISADORA	Miss Maple, how could you be so unfeeling? The poor man is dead.
CYNTHIA	From what I know of his acting reputation the man died on stage many times. At last he managed to put in a convincing performance.
PRATT	I will believe that it was an heart attack when I have post moribund evidence of the fact. Until then, ladies, I will pursue all avenues of enquiry. Has Nurse Peartree completed her examination of the copse?
ISADORA	I don't know, Inspector, I haven't seen her.
PRATT	I see. This is very irregular. I told her to report to me as soon as she'd finished her exhumations.
ISADORA	Perhaps she may return soon, Inspector.
PRATT	Perhaps so, Lady Pillock, perhaps so. *(Shaking his head.)* It saddens me. This whole affair comes as a terrible personal loss.

ISADORA   Really, Inspector?

PRATT   Does that surprise you? I may give the
               impression of a hard hearted professional
               copper whose seen everything . . . done
               everything . . . who's sacrificed his humanity
               for the sake of the job. But I still have feelings.
               Underneath this hard exterior, these broad
               shoulders, I'm still a human bean with feelings
               like any other broad bean.

ISADORA   I'm sure you are. I never doubted it for one
               moment, Inspector.

PRATT   (*picking up the deer stalker fondly*) I first met
               the Colonel several years ago. Since then, I've
               always regarded him as a friend . . . not the sort
               you'd send a Christmas card to but,
               nevertheless, a friend. (*Gazing at the settee.*)
               And now he lies there . . . in a deadly
               condition.

ISADORA   (*uncertain*) The *Colonel's* not actually dead
               you know.

PRATT   (*kindly*) Ah, Lady Pillock, I'm afraid we must
               face reality. We saw him drop to his doom with
               our own eyes.

CYNTHIA   As I explained at the time, Inspector, that was
               Mister Longfellow. He was pretending to be
               Charles. That's why he was here in the first
               place.

PRATT   Longfellow?

CYNTHIA   Yes.

PRATT   (*blustering his way out*) I knew that. I saw
               through his little disguise. (*Thinking hard.*) Of
               course, we must take care. It may all have been
               a cunning plan to deceive us. Maybe it was in
               fact the Colonel, heavily disguised as himself.

CYNTHIA   What a preposterous idea!

ISADORA   In any case nurse could make a positive
               identification. I'm sure she would know if the
               Colonel had any hidden identifying features.

PRATT   Exactly. Such as a card in his wallet

ISADORA   I was thinking he may have something like a
               small mole, Inspector.

PRATT   I see, of course. It's amazing you know . . . you
               think you know someone . . . all these years
               and I never realised that Colonel Herring had a
               pendant for small mammals.

ISADORA   (*standing*) If you'll excuse me, Inspector, I
               think I'll go up to my room for a short while.
               This has all been very tiring. Perhaps you
               might lend me your copy of your sister's
               memoirs, Miss Maple. I'd be very interested to
               glance through them.

CYNTHIA   Of course. Come along, I'll get them for you. I
               don't suppose we're going to salvage anything
               out of this weekend now.

PRATT   On the contrary, Missus Mayday. I fully intend
               to savage the weekend. If either of you should
               see Nurse Peartree, tell her I'd like to see her.

ISADORA   With pleasure.

PRATT   In the meantime I will continue my exhausting
               investigations in here alone.

ISADORA   What are you planning, Inspector?

PRATT   (*knowingly*) Ah, tricks of the trade, Lady
               Pilchard . . . tricks of the trade.

(ISADORA *and* CYNTHIA *exit into the hall
leaving* PRATT *alone. He is bored and has no
idea what to do. He carelessly tosses the deer
stalker onto the "body" and then wanders
aimlessly up and down for a moment. He pulls
out a handkerchief and blows his nose loudly,
inspecting his handkerchief closely before
replacing it in his pocket. He has a sudden
flash of inspiration and moves to the
sideboard, pausing on the way to mimic*
PUCHLIK's *posture with hand on hip. He mimes
pouring a drink and carrying it to where*
CARDEW *was standing when he took the drink
at the end of the previous scene. He mimes
handing the drink to* CARDEW. *He then walks
carefully around to where* CARDEW *was
standing and mimes* CARDEW *taking the drink
and taking a sip of it before silently mouthing
a few words. Suddenly he grasps his throat,
making a gargling noise. He stops and shakes
his head before repeating the whole sequence,
starting from pouring the drink, and ending by
miming a heart attack, this time clutching his
chest and making different gargling noises.
Unable to make his mind up he starts to
alternate between clutching his chest and his
throat. Finally he stops miming and shrugs his
shoulders. He crosses his arms and wanders
around the room aimlessly, bored again.
Unseen by* PRATT, LILY *opens the secret panel
slightly and tries to attract his attention.*)

LILY   (*off, in the secret passageway*) Pssssssst.

(LILY *ducks back out of sight, closing the
secret panel as* PRATT *looks round suddenly.
He has heard something but is not sure what.
He glances around the room in curiosity
before moving closer to the body on the settee
and cupping his hand to his ear to listen
closely. Hearing nothing, he moves away from
the body. He lifts his wrist watch to his ear,
wondering if the noise came from there.
Satisfied, he wanders the room again, turning*

his back to the secret panel. Lily *enters*
through the secret panel, closing it behind her
before hissing at Pratt *again.*)

LILY   Psssst.

                (Pratt *turns in surprise and sees* Lily.)

PRATT   Missus Anthill! How did you do that?

LILY   It were quite easy, sir, I just went "pssssst".

PRATT   I see.

LILY   (*moving to* Pratt *and talking to him*
                confidentially in her serious, educated voice)
                You must be very careful. Things are not all
                that they seem.

PRATT   (*lost*) And how do they seem to you?

LILY   It's best that you know as little as possible. In
                your case that will be an amazingly easy task.
                The important thing is that we give nothing
                away. Not a hint that we know anything.

PRATT   About what?

LILY   I can't tell you. You may go blundering into
                something if you know the truth.

PRATT   I'll have you know that I'm an officer of the law
                . . . an Inspector. It is my prerogative (*He*
                pronounces it perojative.) to blunder whether I
                know the truth or not. People lie deceased . . .
                all around us. I demand to know what's going
                on.

LILY   And I refuse to tell you. I have to think about
                national security.

PRATT
(*sulking*) If you don't tell me I'm going to get very cross. Then where will you be? Anyway, if I don't know anything I may inadvertently open my mouth and let the cat out of the bush.

LILY
I suppose you may be right. All right, I'll tell you one thing. Count Puchlik is an adopted alias. Now remember, it is absolutely vital that you tell no one and that my true identity remains concealed from the others. I can rely on you?

PRATT
Is the Pope a Protestant, Missus Anthill? I guarantee that you can rely on me with your life.

LILY
I hope it won't come to that. Yours is simply a watching brief.

PRATT
My lips are sealed, . . . my tongue is tied.

LILY
Not a word to anyone.

(HENRIETTA *is heard off in the hall*.)

HENRIETTA
I'll be with you in a jiffy, Count. Just got to check in here first.

LILY
(*immediately reverting to her cooks accent*) And don't forget, Inspector, you just tell Missus Pratt that she needs more suet in 'er dumplings.

(HENRIETTA *enters from the hall carrying a clip board and pencil*.)

HENRIETTA
Sorry. Didn't realise anyone was jolly well in here. Didn't mean to barge in.

LILY
Don't worry, love, I was just going. No peace for the wicked. That's one thing about my job. It don't matter 'ow many people's dead; the

ones who are alive'll always be wanting
something to eat. Now, don't you go forgetting
what I said, sir.

PRATT   (*confused*) About Missus Pratt's dumplings?

LILY   No, sir, the other matter. (*To* HENRIETTA.) He is
                 a one with 'is little jokes.

                 (LILLY *exits to the hall.*)

PRATT   (*sadly*) Missus Pratt never makes dumplings.

HENRIETTA   Gosh, we used to have the most tremendous
                 dumpling fights in the school refectory. Used
                 to stick all over the place . . . up the walls, on
                 the ceiling! Matron used to get incredibly
                 maungy about it. Would you excuse me a
                 moment, Inspector? I'm just making an
                 inventory of the rooms.

PRATT   Ah, yes. For your top secret work.

HENRIETTA   Well, it is a bit hush hush. If the balloon goes
                 up, our chaps might have a use for this place.
                 Very isolated, you see, that's the key to it
                 apparently. Prying eyes would be fairly
                 noticeable.

PRATT   (*self important*) Of course I'm used to carrying
                 out top secret work myself, on the force.

                 (*Throughout the following conversation,*
                 HENRIETTA *moves around the room taking
                 notes.*)

HENRIETTA   I expect you are, Inspector. Sounds awfully
                 exciting.

PRATT   Oh yes. If any important under-the-covers work
                 comes along I'm usually the first man on the
                 duty rostrum. The superintendent has often

commented on my amplitude for it. (*Proudly*.)
Only the other day he remarked on it. Pratt, he
said, you function at a level beyond the
comprehension of any other officer on this
force.

HENRIETTA   Oh? That sounds tremendous, Inspector.

PRATT   Oh, yes. (*Confidentially*.) As it happens I'm
             working on something rather hush hush myself
             at the moment. All of this business with the
             housekeeper and Mister Longbottom there is
             purely incidental. I have far bigger fish to fillet.

HENRIETTA   Jolly intriguing. Far more exciting than my
             boring old work. You wouldn't believe the
             amount of paperwork. It's hard to keep one's
             head above water.

PRATT   (*proudly*) Oh, I'm frequently operating way
             over my head. Matters of National import . . .
             and export. Oh, yes. Things are not always as
             they seem. I wouldn't normally talk about
             matters of security but I assume you must have
             the highest level of secular clearance.

HENRIETTA   Absolutely top-notch.

PRATT   You may be of some help perhaps. Maybe see
             something or hear something. I'd make it worth
             your while of course. Might even be a
             promotion in it for you. I'm sure I could pull a
             few strings.

HENRIETTA   Really! Daddy always says I'll never make
             anything of myself. How can I help?

PRATT   (*moving close to* HENRIETTA *and speaking
             confidentially*) I have the gravest of doubts
             about one of the guests. I believe Count
             Pushluck has adopted aliens.

HENRIETTA   He's what!

PRATT	He is not what he appears to be. He may be one of those! Perhaps even one of the others!
HENRIETTA	You don't mean!
PRATT	I think I possibly do.
HENRIETTA	But this is dreadful. Do you want me to report him at my end?
PRATT	No. You must do nothing with your end at the moment. I have my end in hand. You are simply to watch his briefs. We must move cautiously.
HENRIETTA	Very good, Inspector. I'll jolly well do my best. Mum's the word.
PRATT	Is it really?
HENRIETTA	I promise I won't say a word.
PRATT	I know I can rely on you.
HENRIETTA	I think that does it in here. Must move on. (*Glancing at the body on the settee and moving towards it.*) Don't you think we ought to do something with poor Mister Longfellow? It doesn't seem right just leaving him there.
PRATT	Well done . . . I was thinking along those lines myself . . . he is taking up rather a lot of room. Perhaps we could sit him up in a chair or prop him in a corner out of the way.
HENRIETTA	No, I meant move him to another room . . . somewhere quieter where he can lie peacefully. It's rather spooky having him hanging around in here.
PRATT	Very well. Perhaps we could take him upstairs. Of course, wriggley mortise will have taken

hold. We may not be able to bend him round the stairs.

(C<small>ARDEW</small> *enters from the dining room, dressed as* C<small>HARLES</small> *in jacket and tie. From this point on* C<small>ARDEW</small> *always impersonates* C<small>HARLES</small> *unless stage directions state otherwise.*)

C<small>ARDEW</small>   Bend who round the stairs, old boy?

P<small>RATT</small>   Ah, Colonel. We were about to move the copse of this Longbow chap. Perhaps you might give us a hand.

C<small>ARDEW</small>   Course, old boy. Anything to oblige.

(C<small>ARDEW</small> *moves towards the dining room door but pauses as* P<small>RATT</small> *calls him back.*)

P<small>RATT</small>   Where are you going, Colonel?

C<small>ARDEW</small>   To get the chap's body.

P<small>RATT</small>   (*pointing to the body on the settee*) Here, Colonel Herring . . . he's here.

C<small>ARDEW</small>   Oh, get you now. Moved him back did you . . . good show.

P<small>RATT</small>   What do you mean . . . moved him back? This isn't a piece of hand luggage we're dealing with here. It's a copse.

C<small>ARDEW</small>   But I dragged him through into the dining room earlier, old boy. Put him under the table out of the way. I kept tripping over the chap in here.

P<small>RATT</small>   I certainly didn't move him back.

C<small>ARDEW</small>   (*moving to the dining room door and peering through*) Well he's not in here any more.

PRATT   Of course he isn't! He's in here.

HENRIETTA   (*brightly*) I think I've got it.

PRATT   Have you?

HENRIETTA   Somebody else must have moved him.

PRATT   So it would seem. Most irregular. Right,
             Colonel. (*Moving to the settee.*) I'd appreciate
             a hand from you . . . I'll take a foot.

             (CARDEW *moves to the "head" end of the body,*
             PRATT *to the feet.* HENRIETTA *stands behind the
             settee watching.* PRATT *reaches down and
             grabs hold of the shoes. He is surprised when
             the shoes come away in his hand and he looks
             at them for a second before reaching down
             and pulling the sheet off the body to reveal the*
             NURSE *lying there. Taken by surprise,*
             HENRIETTA *screams.* PRATT *faints to the floor.*)

             (*The lights fade and then rise again, denoting
             a short passage in time. The body of the* NURSE
             has been removed. PRATT *is slumped in a chair
             with* ISADORA *standing over him, mopping his
             brow with a cloth.* ISADORA'*s hand bag is lying
             on the settee. A teapot, milk jug and cup and
             saucer are on a wheeled tea trolley by the side
             of the chair.*)

ISADORA   Is that feeling any better, Inspector?

PRATT   Yes, I'm much better, Lady Pilchard. The
             circulation's returning to my head I think.

ISADORA   A cup of tea works wonders. You should take
             things easy for a little while. You've been
             overdoing it.

PRATT   (*in panic*) Take things easy! With a
             psychosomatic maniac on the loose! He could
             be after *me* next!

ISADORA   I don't think you're in any more danger than
               the rest of us, Inspector.

PRATT   Of course I am! I'm the lunchpin of the entire
               investigation. He might think I'll work out who
               the murderer is!

ISADORA   I don't believe anyone would be that stupid,
               Inspector. In any case you can't give in to him.
               It's your duty to carry on and deliver us all.
               We ladies feel so vulnerable. This is the hour
               for valiant men of action like yourself. How I
               wish I had your fortitude.

PRATT   (*flattered*) Oh, it's nothing.

ISADORA   (*stroking his head seductively*) But I'm a mere
               woman. And you're such a . . . strong . . . man.
               Such strength only makes me feel even more
               weak and helpless.

PRATT   (*pulling himself together, preening himself*)
               You're quite right. I shall apprehend the culprit
               if it's the last thing I ever do.

ISADORA   (*moving away, centre*) It's so frightening
               upstairs in our rooms, it rather gives me the
               creeps. The corridors are so gloomy . . . it's like
               a labyrinth full of dark nooks and crannies.
               How can we sleep unless you stay awake
               through the night to protect us?

PRATT   (*standing and moving to* ISADORA) You have
               my word on it. Never fear whilst a Pratt is near.
               You ladies may rest easy in your beds tonight
               knowing that I will be aroused and exploring
               your secret nooks.

ISADORA   I hope you'll be careful, Inspector. We don't
               want any accidents.

PRATT   I am a man of considerable experience, Lady
               Pilchard. I always carry adequate precautions.

(Tapping the revolver in his top jacket pocket reassuringly.) I will be well protected.

ISADORA   I'm so pleased to hear it. Perhaps I may now be able to retire with a sense of ease.

PRATT   *(lightly)* I'd hardly have thought you old enough for that, Lady Pilchard.

ISADORA   For what?

PRATT   To retire.

ISADORA   Oh, . . . I often retire early.

PRATT   You've done it before then?

ISADORA   Of course.

PRATT   Yes, of course.

ISADORA   I'll take my leave then, Inspector.

PRATT   Ah yes, before you've retired. Very good. I have mine booked for July. Myself, the wife and the little Pratts are going to Blackpool for the week.

ISADORA   I'm sorry?

PRATT   There's no need, Lady Pilchard. The little Pratts enjoy it there.

ISADORA   I'm sure you'll have a very nice time. Anyway, I'll go up to my room now, if you'll excuse me.

PRATT   So soon?

ISADORA   As I said, I often retire early.

PRATT   Ah, yes . . . quite.

(ISADORA *picks up her handbag and moves
towards the hall door. She stops abruptly.*)

Oh, Inspector, I nearly forgot. The Colonel
found this down the back of the settee when he
and the Count were removing Nurse Parsley's
poor broken body.

(ISADORA *passes a penknife to* PRATT.)

It seems that it was the implement which was
used to cut her throat.

(PRATT *stares at the penknife in horror.*)

Is something wrong, Inspector? Have you seen
it before?

PRATT   (*casually, starting to feel inside his jacket
pocket*) No . . . no. I was merely internally
hypothecating on the horrendous horror.

ISADORA   What a dreadful death. The poor innocent girl.
Goodnight, Inspector.

PRATT   (*absently*) Goodnight, Lady Piffle.

(ISADORA *exits into the hall.* PRATT *examines
the penknife closely before searching all his
pockets frantically to find his own penknife.
Unable to find it he panics, shifting the
penknife from hand to hand, looking at it in
amazement, then looking around the room
desperately trying to find somewhere to hide
it.*)

(*to himself*) The Chief Super would never
believe it. The lavatory . . . I could flush it
down the lavatory.

(PRATT *exits into the hall hurriedly. As he leaves,* PUCHLIK *enters cautiously from the dining room.*)

PUCHLIK   (*in his German voice*) All is clear. Ze Inspector has left ze room empty.

(PUCHLIK *beckons to* HENRIETTA *who enters from the dining room behind him.*)

Quickly, ve have little time to prepare my cunning plan.

HENRIETTA   (*in her serious voice*) Do you seriously expect this to work.

PUCHLIK   But of course. Ve have no choice other than to exterminate him. It vill give me ze greatest of pleasures to strike ze first blow for ze glorious invasion. Zere vill be von less Britisher for ze panzers to crush mercilessly under zere foots.

HENRIETTA   I know we have to get rid of him. It's the method I'm not sure about.

PUCHLIK   Of course it vill vork. Pass me ze cigar case from ze sideboard.

(*During the following speech* HENRIETTA *fetches the wooden cigar case from the top of the sideboard and returns to* PUCHLIK *by the tea trolley.* PUCHLIK *produces three cigars from his pocket.*)

Ze finest brains in Germany have vorked ceaselessly to produce all the apparatus necessary for ze successful assassin. Here ve have one of zere masterpieces . . .

(PUCHLIK *holds up one of the cigars for* HENRIETTA *to admire.*)

Ze exploding cigar.

HENRIETTA | But the others will be suspicious. What are they going to think when they find him with the remains of a cigar plastered all over his face.

PUCHLIK | Zis is why ve vill win ze var unt you vill lose it so badly. Careful planning is imperative. (*Emptying the cigars from the cigar box into his pocket and replacing them with his own three cigars.*) When ze Inspector is alone, I vill offer him one of ze exploding cigars.

HENRIETTA | What if he doesn't smoke?

PUCHLIK | I have vays of making him smoke. After igniting ze cigar, we vill retire to ze safety of ze adjoining room. Precisely von minute after ze cigar is ignited . . . voosh . . . no more Inspector Pratt. At zis point we vill re-enter zis room, replace ze normal cigars in ze box, smash ze oil lamp next to ze body und start ze large fire. When ze others arrive they vill find us trying to extinguish ze Inspector's flames. Very cunning, ja?

HENRIETTA | I must admit it seems rather faultless.

PUCHLIK | But of course. Ve are ze master-race. We are always faultless.

(PRATT *is heard whistling nonchalantly in the hall.*)

Shhhh . . . now may be our opportunity.

(PUCHLIK *returns the cigar case to the sideboard and remains there. Henrietta moves right. They both act casually. Suddenly, from the hall is the sound of buckets being kicked and crockery falling.*)

PRATT | (*off*) Ah . . . that'll be the cupboard.

(*Seconds later* Pratt *enters from the hall whistling as nonchalantly as he can. He is surprised to find* Puchlik *and* Henrietta *in the room. They both revert to their other accents.* Henrietta *moves to* Pratt.)

HENRIETTA   (*moving to* Pratt) Inspector! Jolly nice of you to join us. We were just thinking of having a little night-cap.

PRATT   Not for me, Captain. Not while I'm on duty. I need to keep an empty head at all times.

(Henrietta *takes* Pratt's *arm and leads him down, out of* Puchlik's *hearing.*)

HENRIETTA   I've been keeping an eye on him for you, Inspector. He's absolutely fine. I don't think you need worry about him, he's definitely absolutely genuine . . . top notch sort of chap.

PRATT   Ah, good. Pleased to hear it . . . much as I thought myself but you can't be too careful. Some of the most ruthless criminals look as though batter wouldn't melt in their mouth.

HENRIETTA   I quite agree . . . absolutely.

PRATT   (*anxiously*) I don't suppose you thought anything was odd when I came in just now.

HENRIETTA   Why should we.

PRATT   (*trying to move casually back up centre*) I just went for a short stroll down the hall . . . to the toilet. Nothing more than that.

PUCHLIK   Am very happy for you, Inspector.

PRATT   Only, I wouldn't want you to think I was doing anything suspicious or underhand. You might have thought that I just wandered off to dispose of something . . . you know, like some important piece of incriminating evidence . . . a penknife perhaps.

PUCHLIK   But you are policeman. Why would we expect such thing?

PRATT   Well, you know how things are. Anyway, it's irreverent because I wasn't and so that's an end to it.

PUCHLIK   Quite so.

(*Carrying the cigar box down towards the tea trolley and offering* PRATT *a cigar from the open box.*)

Would you care for cigar, Inspector.

PRATT   (*moving to join* PUCHLIK *at the tea trolley*) No thank you, Count . . . I don't anymore. Smoke tends to upset Missus Pratt's chest.

PUCHLIK   Such pity, Inspector. Colonel Craddock has fine selection. Take this one for example. (*Taking an exploding cigar from the box and placing the box on the tea trolley.*) Is very special.

PRATT   Is it?

HENRIETTA   Gosh, yes. (*Moving closer to examine it.*) Daddy occasionally manages to get hold of those. Frightfully expensive. Best cigar in the world he always says.

PUCHLIK   Your father is fine judge. Please, Inspector, treat yourself.

PRATT   (*tempted*) I really shouldn't. I keep thinking of Missus Pratt's chest.

HENRIETTA   You may as well while you're not with Missus
              Pratt. While the cat's away?

PRATT   We don't have a cat.

HENRIETTA   I always think a cigar makes a chap look
              tremendously important. All the top people
              smoke them, you know. Makes them look jolly
              commanding.

PRATT   (*attempting a light hearted joke*) A bit like me,
              you mean. I expect it does.

HENRIETTA   I'll bet that you'd look like, oh I don't know, a
              very senior politician or a top ranking civil
              servant.

PRATT   (*flattered*) Really?

PUCHLIK   Hold it, Inspector. Feel quality.

HENRIETTA   Yes, do.

PRATT   Oh, very well.

              (PUCHLIK *hands the cigar to* PRATT *who poses
              with it importantly.*)

HENRIETTA   Oh, yes. Rather. Very impressive.

PRATT   Do you think so?

              (PUCHLIK *glances at* HENRIETTA, *indicating that
              she should check that all is clear outside the
              room. During the following speech she moves
              quickly but casually to check both doors.*)

PUCHLIK   Cigar makes you look like statesman. Smell
              aroma, Inspector. Is very good.

(PRATT *sniffs tentatively at the cigar.* PUCHLIK *glances at* HENRIETTA *who nods reassuringly.* PUCHLIK *takes a lighter from his pocket.*)

Let me light for you, Inspector. Just try.

PRATT   Shouldn't really.

PUCHLIK   Such nonsense. (*Lighting the cigar.*) There, how you like?

PRATT   (*taking a puff*) Mmm. Very nice.

PUCHLIK   Man who does not finish this cigar is man who has lost will to live.

(PRATT *coughs slightly, unconvinced.*)

Excuse me, Inspector. Must spend penny as you say.

PRATT   (*preoccupied with the cigar*) Oh, right.

(PUCHLIK *moves quickly to the dining room door and beckons* HENRIETTA *to join him.*)

HENRIETTA   I'll be back in a mo', Inspector.

(PUCHLIK *and* HENRIETTA *move out of sight into the dining room.* PRATT *continues to pose but is increasingly unconvinced by the cigar and he starts to cough and splutter. He looks at the cigar dubiously and attempts one more puff which starts him coughing and wheezing even more.*)

PRATT   (*to himself, spluttering*) No, I don't think so.

(*He looks around for somewhere to dispose of it and, noticing the tea pot, lifts the lid and drops the cigar inside. He picks another cigar*

out of the box and stands posing with it,
pleased with himself.)

PRATT   (*to himself, still clearing his throat, satisfied*)
                 That's better.

                 (PUCHLIK'S *head peers round the door from the*
                 dining room. He sees PRATT *with the cigar and*
                 smiles happily to himself before drawing back
                 out of sight as CYNTHIA *enters from the hall.*)

CYNTHIA   Ah, it's you, Inspector.

PRATT   (*posing importantly*) It is indeed.

                 (*Throughout the following,* PRATT *tries to*
                 impress CYNTHIA *by adopting more and more*
                 exaggerated statesman-like poses. She does
                 not pay any attention to them and he becomes
                 increasingly frustrated.)

CYNTHIA   (*moving to* PRATT) Well, I didn't want you. I
                 was wanting to have words with the Colonel . . .
                 have you seen him?

PRATT   Not for some time, Missus Mayday.

CYNTHIA   Hmmm. Very inconvenient.

                 (CYNTHIA *glances around with a frown.*)

                 This whole weekend has turned into a total
                 disaster. How will I ever work again! I have
                 standards, Inspector and I feel as though I've
                 been badly let down by all of this. (*Noticing*
                 the tea trolley.) Look, he's even allowing the
                 place itself to go downhill. Whatever is Missus
                 Tuthill thinking of, leaving finished crockery
                 lying around. (*Pushing the trolley over to and*
                 through the dining room door.) I shall have
                 words with her. There is no excuse for allowing
                 standards to drop, even in these trying
                 circumstances.

(CYNTHIA *pushes the trolley just out of sight before having second thoughts and moving quickly back to* PRATT.)

If you see the Colonel would you tell him that I wish to see him urgently?

PRATT

It will be my pleasure, Missus Mayday.

CYNTHIA

Thank you. I shall be in the lounge.

(CYNTHIA *exits into the hall.* PRATT *continues to practice his posing.* PUCHLIK'S *and* HENRIETTA'S *heads appear around the dining room door. They have their fingers in their ears. They watch* PRATT *eagerly. After a moment,* HENRIETTA *sniffs the air.*)

HENRIETTA

(*quietly to* PUCHLIK) Can you smell something?

PUCHLIK

(*quietly, also sniffing*) I think I can smell ze cigar smoke.

(*Both of their heads disappear from view.*)

(*off*) It vould appear that ze teapot is smoking. This is very unusual, ja? I shall open it und see vat is happening. (*Pause.*) Ah . . . zis is not good.

(*There is a loud explosion off in the dining room.* PRATT *ducks down onto his knees. There is complete silence from the dining room.*)

PRATT

Hello? . . . hello, there . . . is anybody there?

(PRATT *moves slowly and cautiously to the dining room door. He stands in the doorway looking at the scene inside with amazement. Suddenly his attention is caught by something and he looks upward towards the dining room ceiling.*)

Ah . . . Captain. You appear to be in my bedroom? (*Looking suddenly downwards.*) And in the cellar!

(*The lights fade and rise again denoting a passage of time.*)

(*Several minutes later.* PUCHLIK *is sitting on the settee looking very stunned. His face is blackened and his hair is standing on end.* ISADORA *and* CYNTHIA *are seated on the chairs.* LILY *stands behind the settee and* CARDEW *stands behind the chairs. He continues to impersonate* CHARLES. PRATT *paces the floor.*)

PRATT   (*taking notes*) And then what happened, Count Pushyourluck?

PUCHLIK   I entered dining room. Captain Henrietta is there. Suddenly is big vroom noise and Captain Henrietta is not there. Instead there is big hole in ceiling and floor. I fall through floor.

PRATT   And you have no idea what caused the vroom to occur?

PUCHLIK   I can only make guess, Inspector. Maybe Captain has secret military equipment which accidentally go off.

PRATT   That is a strong possibility, Count. And having gone off it would then perhaps be unstable and explode without warning. (*To them all in general.*) I think that solves that one then. Captain Wooley-Cardigan accidentally blew herself into several rooms due to the vroom . . . a tragic accident.

CYNTHIA   I think there may be more to it than that.

PRATT   Oh I see. And you suddenly know more about my job than I do . . . do you do? Do you?

CYNTHIA   Have you taken the trouble to examine the dining room, Inspector?

PRATT   Of course I have.

CYNTHIA   And it seems you discovered nothing of value?

PRATT   Ah well, that's where you're wrong, Missus Mayday. (*Proudly producing small silver salt and pepper pots from his pocket.*) As it happens I found this rather expensive silver suet set which will go very nicely with Missus Pratt's best china.

(PRATT *smiles at them all contentedly. They look at him in amazement.*)

CARDEW   That's mine, old boy! What are you doing with it in your pocket?

PRATT   In my pocket! Ah! I was wondering when you'd ask that. Very good, Colonel . . . very good indeed. It is in my pocket because . . . it is evidence. Very, very important evidence which I have to keep in my pocket for safe keeping.

(PRATT *hurriedly replaces the salt and pepper pots back in his pocket.*)

CYNTHIA   Did you take the trouble to examine the remains of the tea trolley?

PRATT   Of course I did.

CYNTHIA   And what did you discover?

PRATT   It was very bent and one wheel was quite wobbly.

CYNTHIA   Did you notice anything in particular about the tea pot, Inspector?

PRATT   I might have . . . (*Consulting his notebook
             hopefully.*) or I might not have. A good
             detective is never bound by convectional
             methods.

CYNTHIA   Well, Inspector?

PRATT   Ah, I have it now. (*Guessing.*) The spout was a
             little bent?

CYNTHIA   The spout, Inspector, was embedded in the
             Captain's head. The rest of the teapot was
             apparently missing, until I took the trouble to
             examine the walls. Tiny pieces of the teapot
             were embedded in all four walls. Surely you
             noticed that!

PRATT   I did notice that the plaster had a rather
             attractive decorative texture.

CARDEW   Good, Lord! That means the tea pot must have
             been at the epicentre of the explosion, old boy.

CYNTHIA   Exactly.

PRATT   You mean it was . . . ? (*Totally lost.*) Very good.
             And exactly what makes you such an expert
             Missus Mayhem?

CYNTHIA   I make my living from creating and recreating
             crime, Inspector. I examined the remains of the
             teapot very carefully. It really wasn't
             tremendously difficult to piece it all together.

PRATT   On the contrary, I would say that the tea pot is
             irreparable. But thank you for your vigilance.
             Perhaps the rest of you might take a leaf out of
             Missus Mayhem's tree. It's everyone's duty to
             aid and abet the police. If Missus Mayhem
             hadn't been such a vigilante she wouldn't have
             been able to confirm my secret theory.

ISADORA   Which is what, Inspector?

PRATT	That this was a text book case of an exploding tea pot accident. I've seen it before. Pensioners sat by the fireside with a cuppa and a currant bun and suddenly, vroom, they're gone. Very unpredictable. It certainly wouldn't have anything to do with someone putting a lighted cigar inside the teapot. You're all free to go about your business for the rest of the evening.
CARDEW	You can't be serious, old boy. That can't be it.
PRATT	Do you have a better explanation, Colonel Kipper?
CARDEW	Well, yes . . . no, I don't suppose I have. Never heard of an exploding tea pot though! Dashed queer if you ask me.
LILY	Well, if that's all finished with, would someone 'elp me take the poor Polish gentleman up to 'is room for a lie down. He doesn't look very well to me.
PUCHLIK	Is all right. I will be, as you say, tickety-boo. Like United States of America I have fine constitution. See, I even make joke.
CARDEW	United States? Dashed colonials. Did I ever tell you about the time I was in Washington DC . . .
PRATT	Inspector.
CARDEW	What, old boy?
PRATT	You said DC . . . detective constable. I'm a detective Inspector.
CARDEW	No, no. DC as in Washington DC. I must've told you the story!
PUCHLIK	You never tell me but am sure you will. Suddenly I feel not so good any more.

PRATT   I'll give you a hand, Missus Hilltop.

LILY   I'll go on in front, sir and get the gentleman's
               room open.

PUCHLIK   Is no need.

LILY   I think there is, sir, you're very weak.

               (LILY *exits into the hall leaving the door
               slightly ajar.* CARDEW *watches from the
               sideboard.*)

PRATT   Come along, sir.

               (PRATT *holds* PUCHLIK'S *left arm and helps him
               to his feet. He guides him to the hall door.*
               PUCHLIK *is still very dazed and is not capable
               of walking unaided. As they reach the door,*
               PRATT *opens the door which strikes* PUCHLIK,
               knocking him sideways towards the sideboard.
               CARDEW *catches him.* PRATT *continues out of
               sight into the hall, before reappearing in the
               doorway, realising that he has lost* PUCHLIK.
               *He glances around the room in confusion
               before seeing* PUCHLIK *slumped up against the
               sideboard with* CARDEW *supporting him.* PRATT
               grabs hold of PUCHLIK *and finally manages to
               help him out towards the hall.*)

PRATT   Come along . . . you don't need another drink,
               sir!

               (PRATT *and* PUCHLIK *exit into the hall.*)

CYNTHIA   How ridiculous, he won't get him anywhere at
               that rate. I've never seen anything like it.

               (CYNTHIA *exits into the hall, calling after
               them.*)

               I'll help you up the stairs, Inspector.

PRATT   (*off*) No need, Missus Mayhem, I can manage
                        him.

                        (*There is the sound off of* PUCHLIK *crying out
                        and falling down the stairs.*)

                        (*off*) Sorry.

                        (CARDEW *and* ISADORA *are left alone in the
                        room.* CARDEW *moves to the sideboard and
                        starts to help himself to a whisky.* ISADORA
                        remains seated.)

CARDEW   Bit of a rum do, all of this. Can't for the life of
                        me work out what's going on. Bad form all
                        these chaps dropping all over the place. Can I
                        get you a drink, Lady Pollock?

                        (ISADORA *remains silent.*)

                        I said can I get you a drink?

                        (ISADORA *remains silent and* CARDEW *moves
                        down centre with his whiskey in his hand.*)

                        I say, old girl, are you all right? Here's me
                        rambling on without a thought. Perhaps you'd
                        best go for a lie down or something, you're
                        looking a bit pale.

ISADORA   (*coldly, in an accent which has none of her
                        usual refinement*) You don't remember me do
                        you?

CARDEW   Course I do. You're Lady Isadora Pollock. I
                        know I'm a bit of a duffer sometimes but I'm
                        not senile yet . . . well on my way mind but not
                        quite there yet!

ISADORA   I mean from before. You don't remember me
                        from before.

CARDEW   Before what, old girl?

ISADORA   Don't call me that. You used to call your wife,
              old girl. She hated it. She told me.

CARDEW   No offence meant. Just an expression. Should I
              know you?

ISADORA   You may have seen my photograph. You
              certainly knew my husband.

CARDEW   Did I? Pollock . . . Pollock . . . don't remember
              the name.

ISADORA   (*standing*) His name wasn't Pollock, you fool.
              It's not my name either. His name was Willis . . .
              Private Harry Willis.

CARDEW   Sorry, still not with you.

ISADORA   You killed him.

CARDEW   Now look here, old girl, I think this has gone
              far enough. Never killed anyone like that in my
              life . . . not a Willis. Plenty of foreign chaps but
              all above board, line of duty sort of thing.

ISADORA   Oh you didn't actually pull the trigger but you
              gave the orders. You and your sort. You were
              second in command. You gave him a gun and
              you sent him over the top when you knew he
              wouldn't stand a chance.

CARDEW   Ah . . . get you now . . . now I follow your drift.
              I'm sorry but I don't see the point of this.
              Dashed bad luck but it was a war . . . chaps got
              killed I'm afraid.

ISADORA   They never even found his body. It's like he
              never existed. As far as people like you were
              concerned he didn't matter. Just another
              statistic.

CARDEW   It wasn't easy for any of us you know. But it was a long time ago . . . twenty odd years. Why should I have seen your photograph?

ISADORA   After my trial it was in the newspapers. War widow kills commanding officer. They said I was ill. (*Moving across in front of* CARDEW, *in front of the settee.*) I've been in the asylum ever since . . . until they let me out earlier this year. They said I was better. It was in there that I met your wife. That's how I found out where you were. (*Reaching casually into her bag and producing a revolver.*) She and I had lots of things in common. We both want to kill you.

CARDEW   I'm told she's just escaped.

ISADORA   Hard luck. I got here first.

CARDEW   Are you responsible for all this business! All of these deaths?

ISADORA   Of course not. Only a mad person would do that and my release papers say I'm not mad anymore. I came here because I wanted to find out what you were really like. Your not as bad as I thought you'd be . . . but I've got to go through with it for Harry. This murder weekend has been quite entertaining. Funny but I can't quite work out what's real and what isn't. (*Levelling the revolver at his chest.*) I don't suppose it matters anymore.

CARDEW   Look, we can talk it over. There's something you should know.

ISADORA   Sorry . . . too late.

(ISADORA *pulls the trigger but there is a click as the gun misfires. She tries again and there is another click.* ISADORA *screams with rage, throws the revolver to the floor and picks up*

*the candle stick from the coffee table down
right. She advances threateningly towards
CARDEW who backs away towards the secret
panel.)*

CARDEW   (*panicking*) Look, I'm not . . .

          (CARDEW'S *voice trails off and he clutches at
          his chest.*)

          I'm not . . .

          (ISADORA *moves towards* CARDEW *with the
          candle stick raised to hit him. Before she can
          strike him, he slumps to his knees, then drops
          forward and lies motionless on the floor.*
          ISADORA *laughs at him. As he hits the floor the
          secret panel opens and* CYNTHIA *steps into the
          room. As she enters, the realisation of what
          she sees before her sinks home slowly.*)

CYNTHIA   What! What have you done?

ISADORA   (*laughing maniacally*) I got here first.

CYNTHIA   You've killed him!

          (ISADORA'S *laugh becomes even more manic.*)

          (*flying into a rage*) You fool. You damn fool.
          You've ruined everything . . . everything!

          (CYNTHIA *lunges at* ISADORA *and snatches the
          candle stick from* ISADORA'S *grasp.* ISADORA
          flees out into the hall, laughing again, with
          CYNTHIA *in pursuit.*)

CYNTHIA   (*as she exits*) When I get hold of you you're
          dead. Do you hear me . . . dead.

          (*The lights fade and the curtains close.*)

Scene Two

It is early the following morning. The door to the dining room is slightly ajar. Cynthia *is seated on the settee with* Lily *standing behind the settee.* Pratt *is standing centre stage.*

Pratt   (*consulting his notebook*) And you say that Lady Pillock was standing over his body?

Cynthia   Yes. I came in and found her like that.

Pratt   And she was holding a . . . (*Peering closely at his notes.*) . . . a canned chick!

Cynthia   Candle stick, Inspector. I told you all of this last night.

Pratt   And you can tell me again this morning. I was taking notes in very gloomy light. I just want to be sure of the facts.

Cynthia   There's hardly that much to have to remember.

Pratt   (*trying to read his notes again*) So . . . she was standing over the kindled biddy and you said "You've grilled him". Is that right?

Cynthia   (*tersely*) She was standing over the Colonel's body and I said "You've killed him".

Pratt   Ah, there you are, you see. Already you're changing your story. I knew we'd make progress.

Cynthia   I'm not changing anything. She killed him . . . I know she did. If you hadn't lost his body you'd have the evidence.

Pratt   I haven't lost his body. I've simply misplaced it for the moment. In fact we only have your word that there was a body! You say there was

somebody's body but perhaps there was
nobody's body.

CYNTHIA   Why would I make it up, Inspector? She ran
into the hall and I went after her. She ran down
the hall and out through the front door.
Unfortunately as she ran outside, something
fell out of an upstairs window and struck her
on the head.

PRATT   Unfortunate indeed. (*Consulting notes again.*)
And when you examined her she was tone
deaf?

CYNTHIA   Stone dead.

PRATT   I see.

LILY   If you 'adn't knocked that big vase off the
Count's window sill she'd still be alive,
Inspector.

PRATT   I was merely being helpful, Missus Hilltop . . .
the Count needed fresh air to help him over the
shock of the exploding teapot. I caught the
vase with my elbow . . . a carelessly positioned
vase I might add. Whoever placed it there is
guilty of gross negligees.

CYNTHIA   So that leaves four of us still alive, Inspector.

PRATT   What are you implying?

CYNTHIA   I suppose what I'm implying is that yesterday
afternoon there were ten of us. Under the very
nose of a police Inspector, six people have
died. Not a tremendously good record perhaps.

PRATT   Very unfortunate, yes, but I'm sure that the
superintendent will understand. I have been
suffering from a lot of sinus trouble lately.

CYNTHIA   And you really haven't got the faintest idea
                what's going on have you? Not a single clue.

PRATT   Ah . . . well, that's where you're wrong,
                Missus Maybe. I have been collecting facts
                and . . . (*Waving his notebook*.) . . . all the facts
                are recorded in here. I think if we interrogate
                those facts, I can piece together a pretty
                convincing case against the miscreant.

CYNTHIA   I can't wait.

PRATT   I'll bet you can't, Missus Maybe, I bet you
                can't. Why don't you take a seat, Missus
                Hilltop.

LILY   I will if you like, I suppose.

                (LILY *sits on the settee next to* CYNTHIA.)

PRATT   Right. Let us examine my little catalogue (*He
                pronounces it catalogyou*.) of facts.

                (*Throughout the following speeches he
                frequently refers to his notebook and walks
                around the room indicating where the
                actual events took place. As he realises where
                the facts are leading him he becomes
                increasingly agitated*.)

                Let us start with the housekeeper, Missus
                Headstrong. I was the last person to see her
                before dinner last night. When we came out of
                dinner she was dead. Whilst I suspected an
                heart attack I am prepared to keep an open
                mind about the scissors.

CYNTHIA   Which had been forcibly thrust into her back.

PRATT   As I said, the position of the scissors is not
                open or shut, although they were indeed shut.

CYNTHIA	Would you just get on with it, Inspector!
PRATT	Get on with what?
CYNTHIA	You were reviewing your catalogue. (*She pronounces it the same way as* PRATT.)
PRATT	I hadn't forgotten. (*Pausing for effect.*) Later that evening . . . (*Scathing.*) during the course of your half-baked pasty . . . I handed Cardew Longshanks a drink which he drunk. Having drunk the drink he immediately dropped dead. Natural causes or poison? Perhaps pearshaped Nurse may have been able to tell us but she was later found with her throat cut by a penknife.
CYNTHIA	(*caustically*) Pity you didn't find out who the penknife belonged to.
PRATT	(*smug*) Ah, but I did . . . I did. Don't underestimate me, Missus Maybe. The penknife belonged to me.
CYNTHIA	Really, Inspector?
PRATT	Oh yes.
CYNTHIA	(*raising her eye brows*) Oh dear!
PRATT	Moving on. We then have the epistle of the exploding tea pot which mortified Captain Woolly-Cardigan.
CYNTHIA	Which is still somewhat of a mystery to you I assume.
PRATT	I think not, Missus Maybe. As you know, I had previously been using the tea pot for the purpose of taking tea.
CYNTHIA	Naturally.

PRATT

It is my theory that I inadvertently created an explosive comical reaction within the brew. As Colonel Herring later observed, this caused the teapot to become epileptic. The result is plastered all over the remains of the dining room for all to see. Finally we have the deaths of Colonel Herring and Lady Isabella Pillow as we have just reviewed. A tragic catalogue of events.

CYNTHIA

So what is your conclusion, Inspector?

PRATT

(*gravely*) In view of the overwhelming evidence it appears that I have very little option open to me. (*Looking down at* LILY.) Nobody is above the law, Missus Maybe, and the full weight of that law must now be set in motion.

CYNTHIA

So?

PRATT

(*turning away from* LILY) Inspector George Algernon Pratt. I arrest me on suspicion of three counts of murder and two counts of manslaughter. I do not have to say anything but anything I do say may be taken down and used in evidence against me. I'll accompany myself to the police station as soon as the weather permits.

CYNTHIA

The snow is melting rapidly, Inspector. I'm sure you'll be able to be on your way very soon.

PRATT

I shall be pleading innocent of all charges of course. In view of the gravity of the offences perhaps you would care to rummage through my equipment and handcuff me, Missus Maybe.

CYNTHIA

You have a pair in your car I assume?

PRATT   I rarely find time to eat fruit, Missus Maybe . . .
             but you will find some handcuffs in there.

CYNTHIA   (*standing*) I'll get them, Inspector. It would
             give me great pleasure.

LILY   (*in her serious professional voice*) Sit down
             Miss Maple.

CYNTHIA   (*looking at* LILY *in surprise*) What? Who do
             you think you're talking to?

LILY   (*stern*) I said sit down!

             (CYNTHIA *sits down again in surprise.*)

             (*standing and removing her cooks apron*) I
             think this nonsense has gone far enough,
             Inspector.

PRATT   There is no nonsense, I am simply doing my
             job.

LILY   To your usual standard it appears. Whilst
             Count Puchlik is still recovering in bed . . . I
             took the precaution of locking him in by the
             way . . . I think we can settle matters quite
             safely. I interpret things rather differently,
             Inspector.

PRATT   I see. (*Hopefully.*) You mean I may be innocent
             after all?

LILY   You are most certainly guilty, Inspector, but
             only of incompetence. Let us start with the
             most recent death. You can rest assured,
             Inspector, that the vase missed Lady Pollock.

PRATT   But she had a very large dent in the top of her
             head!

LILY

Caused by a candle stick wielded by Miss Maple.

CYNTHIA

What poppycock.

LILY

Not at all . . . simple fact.

CYNTHIA

(*suspicious*) Who are you?

LILY

Let's just say that I work for the government.

CYNTHIA

It doesn't matter who you work for, you can't prove anything. I was a witness. I saw the whole thing happen . . . I went outside after her and the vase dropped on her head.

LILY

But I have another witness who saw you hit her with the candlestick.

CYNTHIA

You can't have!

LILY

But I have. The reason why the body of the Colonel is missing, is that there never was a body . . . he wasn't dead. When you chased Isadora Pollock out of the room he jumped to his feet and followed you.

CYNTHIA

No!

LILY

Except it wasn't actually the Colonel at all was it, Miss Maple?

CYNTHIA

Of course it was.

LILY

It was Mr Longfellow *pretending* to be the Colonel. (*Walking to the hall door and throwing it open.*) Would you care to join us Mister Longfellow?

(PRATT *gasps as* CARDEW *enters with a theatrical flourish.* CARDEW *no longer impersonates* Charles. *He is dressed in white shirt, cape and cravat.*)

CARDEW   I bid hearty greetings to one and to all.

PRATT   It's you!

CARDEW   It is indeed, good sir.

PRATT   I didn't poison you?

CARDEW   Indeed not. I am very much alive and in the rudest of health.

LILY   Perhaps you might explain to Inspector Pratt what happened when you were attacked by Isadora Pollock.

CARDEW   Ah, yes indeed. What a terribly tortured soul. (*Demonstrating the way in which he backed away from* ISADORA.) When she advanced upon me with murderous intent I could see that no words would quell her anguish. Calling upon my many years experience on the stage (*Dropping to one knee, clutching his ches*t.) I performed with alacrity a most convincing death scene of audacious proportions. How an audience would have roared in approval . . . (*Standing.*) I was magnificent.

LILY   When you saw Mister Longfellow on the floor, you thought that all of your plans had been ruined. You flew into a rage and killed Isadora.

CYNTHIA   I don't know what you're talking about. What plans?

LILY   It really is futile to lie, Miss Maple. We have all the evidence we need from Mister Longfellow. Why don't you start from the beginning?

CYNTHIA   (*to* CARDEW) What have you told them!

CARDEW   Alas, good Lady, your number is, so to speak, well and truly up.

CYNTHIA   Fool! (*Realising that all is lost.*) Very well. When I first met Longfellow my first thought was that he would be very useful for creating an astounding mystery. His resemblance to Colonel Craddock was amazing.

CARDEW   Sadly you became too greedy, Miss Maple.

CYNTHIA   I only wanted what I deserve. I suddenly saw an opportunity to become rich . . . and why not! (*Standing and moving centre stage.*) I approached Mister Longfellow with a scheme. In the course of our little charade last night you were all to believe that Mister Longfellow made the first appearance and suffered a heart attack. In fact, I told the Colonel that he must make the first entrance. He was like a lamb to the slaughter. (*Walking through the events, miming.*) If you remember, Inspector, I took the glass from you and passed it to the Colonel. Concealed between my fingers I had a small phial of an untraceable poison which I broke into the drink. The Colonel died. The plan was for Mister Longfellow to impersonate him for long enough to sell this place and give me half the proceeds. We could both have then gone our own ways . . . considerably richer!

                (PRATT *sits on one of the chairs. Throughout the following explanations he takes notes and alternates between being totally lost and nodding sagely, pretending he knew what was happening. Eventually though, he is reduced to crossing out page after page of notes in his notebook.*)

CARDEW   An attractive proposition, madam. And one which I accepted gladly.

CYNTHIA   See? He's as much to blame as me!

LILY

Sadly for you, Miss Maple, before you made
him your little offer I had already recruited him
to serve his country.

CYNTHIA

What!

LILY

I came to Bagshot House as cook a short while
ago. I was really here to keep an eye on Count
Puchlik, or should I say Heinrich Kuchler. We
knew that he was a spy and that he had come
here to get close to Colonel Craddock.

CYNTHIA

Why would he do that? The Colonel was no
use to anyone.

LILY

The Colonel always played the incompetent old
fool but actually he was a most accomplished
soldier . . . one of the foremost authorities on
the German army in this country. Kuchler knew
that when war came the Colonel would be
heavily involved in shaping Britain's strategic
plans. Plans that would be desperately useful
to Germany. We were going to give Kuchler
what he wanted. Feed him misinformation via
the Colonel. As you will appreciate,
misinformation is a very useful weapon.

CYNTHIA

So why recruit Longfellow here?

LILY

When I first saw Mister Longfellow I realised
what a huge asset he could be. He could spend
the war leading Kuchler a merry dance, here
there and everywhere. The Colonel could be
hidden away and concentrate solely on the real
work. The problem was that Kuchler also met
Mister Longfellow, so he knew that there was a
potential double. Kuchler might eventually
have become suspicious. You solved our
problem. When you suggested your little
scheme to Mister Longfellow I realised it was
perfect. Kuchler would actually witness the
death of the Colonel's double.

CYNTHIA	But I killed the Colonel! I put poison in his drink!

LILY   No, we did a swap. You put clear water into what you *thought* was the Colonel's drink. In actual fact Mister Longfellow *did* make the first entrance in the pastiche. He gave another one of his fine death scenes.

CARDEW (*moving to the settee and sitting*) I drew heavily on my Shakespearean experience for that particular performance.

CYNTHIA The Colonel's still alive!

LILY   And kicking. The plan was to whisk him straight away from here but the snow put paid to that.

CYNTHIA Very clever. But what about the other deaths? You were rather slow there!

LILY   Sadly, yes. Nurse Parsley was a threat to your plan wasn't she? She was the one person who might recognise that you'd killed the Colonel, not Longfellow.

PRATT   Lady Pillows said so at the time. She said he might have a vole.

CYNTHIA Yes, the nurse was a danger. I had to get rid of her first. Unfortunately, at the first attempt I killed Missus Armstrong by accident. It was her fault. She had her back to me and she was wearing the nurses cape. You didn't even notice, Inspector.

PRATT   (*indignant*) I did. I know a nurse's cape when I see one.

CYNTHIA I stabbed her with the scissors but she nearly escaped from me. Fortunately I still managed to

make my way into the dining room before
Inspector Pratt.

LILY   If I'd realised what was going on I could have
            saved Nurse Parsley. As it was, you killed her
            later the same evening.

CYNTHIA   With the Inspector's penknife. I thought that
            was a rather nice touch.

PRATT   (*standing*) I hope you realise that you are in
            very big trouble, Miss Mayhap. Theft of an
            officer's personal equipment is a very serious
            matter!

LILY   I rather think that is of fairly minor importance,
            Inspector.

PRATT   Not to me it isn't! That penknife was a
            Christmas present! (*Moving to* LILY.) But all of
            this confirms the theories that I have had all
            along. I lacked the concrete evidence. It's a
            pity you didn't confide in me earlier Missus
            Hillock. There is just one thing I don't
            understand.

LILY   You surprise me, Inspector.

PRATT   I sometimes surprise myself. (*To* CYNTHIA.)
            Why did you booby trap the tea pot to kill
            Captain Woolly-Cardigan.

CYNTHIA   I didn't.

PRATT   Come now. You don't expect me to believe that.
            I wasn't born yesterday, you know . . . I was
            born on my birthday.

LILY   But she's right, Inspector.

PRATT   What?

LILY   She had nothing to do with it. It was Henrietta and Kuchler.

PRATT   Who blew themselves up! That was rather stupid.

LILY   They were trying to blow *you* up, Inspector.

PRATT   Me!

LILY   Unfortunately it seems to have gone wrong somehow.

PRATT   What do you mean, unfortunately?

LILY   Unfortunately for them.

PRATT   Ah well . . . I out-whittled them. I cleverly turned the stables on them. It's just a pity I didn't get them both.

LILY   On the contrary, we needed to keep Kuchler alive at all costs.

PRATT   (*smiling proudly*) Yes, I knew that. But at least I got his evil accomplice.

LILY   Henrietta was my most skilled agent. It took her six months to gain Kuchler's trust.

PRATT   (*gravely*) Tragic loss.

            (CYNTHIA *starts to laugh and sits on one of the chairs.*)

            This is no laughing matter, Missus Mishap.

CYNTHIA   You don't see, do you . . . you really don't see!

PRATT   I see everything. I have the all-seeing eyes of a bat.

CYNTHIA	Henrietta allowed Kuchler to try to kill you. She probably even helped him!
PRATT	Exactly. Wait a minute . . . (*To* LILY.) You just said she was on our side.
LILY	My apologies. It was not an easy decision, Inspector.
PRATT	What wasn't?
LILY	That you were expendable. We felt, given all the circumstances, that it was in the best interests of the country.
PRATT	To spend me!
LILY	I do have to say that you rather brought it on yourself by being over talkative. We had to shut you up somehow. Then we realised that it was a superb opportunity to cement Henrietta's position of trust with Kuchler.
PRATT	You were going to let them kill me!
LILY	In times of national crisis, sacrifices inevitably have to be made. Look on the bright side, Inspector . . . you would have been a hero.
PRATT	Would I? Yes, I would wouldn't I. (*Puffing his chest out.*) Serving my country like a true Pratt. It would have been an honour.
CYNTHIA	I'm sure you'd be of more service to your country dead than alive.
PRATT	Right . . . that's enough . . . I've had enough of you now. Would you get the handcuffs out of my car, Mister Littlefellow?
CARDEW	What? Yes, of course, we must manacle the good lady.

(Rising, CARDEW *exits into the hall.)*

PRATT   Exactly. We'll see how you like being mangled, Missus Mishap. You just watch your step.

LILY   Sadly, I still don't really understand why you did it, Miss Maple. You had a good name, a fine reputation. To throw it all away like this!

CYNTHIA   I'd had enough. I've spent half my life making a living out of the reputation of that stupid sister of mine. This was a chance to do something in my own right.

LILY   But why go through with your plan in front of so many people? You could have killed the Colonel when it was quieter. You could still have substituted Mister Longfellow in his place.

CYNTHIA   Where would have been the fun in that? I have professional pride. I had it all planned. It would have been the perfect crime. What's the use in carrying out the perfect crime in private . . . I wanted an audience.

PRATT   There's no such thing as the perfect crime. There'll always be clues for a cunning old fox like me to prise out of the wood-worm. Not much escapes my close deliveration.

*(*CHARLES *enters through the secret panel, closing it behind him. He is dressed in an open necked white shirt without a jacket.* PRATT *watches him, open mouthed. Through the following few speeches he stares at the wall, trying to come to terms with the secret panel.)*

LILY   Colonel. Nice of you to join us.

CHARLES   Now then, old girl, just thought I'd pop in and see how things were going.

LILY   Have you checked on our German friend?

CHARLES   Just stuck my nose in. Chap's still flat out on his bed. Been nice to get out and about and stretch my legs while he's cooped up. You've been making a spot of mischief, Cynthia . . . bad form.

CYNTHIA   It was nothing personal, Colonel. I just wanted your money.

CHARLES   Hmmm . . . well you can't have it, old girl . . . it's mine.

PRATT   (*pointing in amazement at the secret panel*) There's a secret door!

CHARLES   (*looking around in surprise*) Where, old boy?

PRATT   Behind you.

CHARLES   Is there? (*Closely studying the wall both sides of the secret panel.*) Where?

PRATT   You just came through it!

CHARLES   Did I? Oh, that! That's not a secret door.

PRATT   Yes it is.

CHARLES   It can't be.

PRATT   Why not?

CHARLES   Everybody knows about it.

PRATT   Well, I didn't, Colonel.

CHARLES   Did I not show it to you? Fancy that! It takes you straight onto the corridor by the lavatory. Saves a bit of time in an emergency if you get my drift.

PRATT   But it's hidden.

CHARLES   Not really ... more disguised, old boy.
                 Architect chap who designed this place
                 thought a door there rather spoilt the cut of the
                 room so he had it built into the panel-work.
                 Made quite a nice job of it. Anyway, best get
                 on. Hear you made a bit of a mess of it all
                 again, old boy.

PRATT   No I didn't.

CHARLES   Like last time. You want to give it up, old boy.
                 You're not cut out for this police business.

PRATT   Don't you be so sure, Colonel. One more word
                 and I may be forced to examine more closely
                 your relationship with small furry animals!

CHARLES   What on earth are you on about?

PRATT   Our little secret, Colonel, our little secret. I
                 never really thought you were dead of course.
                 (*Putting his hand in his pocket he suddenly
                 realises he has the spare cigar in there.*) I was
                 just playing along. (*Pulling the cigar from his
                 pocket.*) Perhaps you'd care for a celebratory
                 cigar, Colonel, for old times sake?

                 (CHARLES *pauses and examines the cigar,
                 nodding in approval.*)

CHARLES   Jolly nice of you, old boy. Don't mind if I do.

                 (CHARLES *exits whistling.*)

PRATT   You know, Missus Hillock, I've been thinking
                 about that attempt on my life. It occurs to me
                 that it must have been some sort of explosive
                 device.

LILY   They're usually the sort of things that go
            bang, yes.

PRATT   I have a hypotenuse. I think the teapot was
            just a decoy. I suspect that they may have
            used an exploding sugar lump.

LILY   I think not. I'm not an expert but for that large
            an explosion it would need a bigger charge.

PRATT   Mmmm, as I thought. How big would you
            think?

LILY   Oh, I don't know. Probably about the same size
            as that cigar.

PRATT   Mmmm . . . ah. (*Slowly realising.*) In fact, what
            you're saying is that a cigar would perhaps do
            it.

LILY   I suppose it would be possible to construct
            something that looked like a cigar.

PRATT   Ah.

LILY   (*suddenly suspicious*) What have you done!

PRATT   (*innocently*) Nothing . . . nothing at all.

            (PRATT *suddenly rushes to the hall door and
            exits. Just as he disappears from view there is
            the sound of an explosion off left.*)

            (*a few seconds after the explosion has died
            down, shouting off*) Sorry . . . sorry.

            (PRATT *enters looking sheepish.*)

            Sorry.

            (LILY *glares at* PRATT *and is about to move to
            the hall door when* CARDEW *staggers in, his*

face blackened with smoke. He has removed
his cravat and cape and is dressed as CHARLES
was in open necked white shirt. He is carrying
CHARLES'S *shoes which are smoking.*)

CARDEW   (*impersonating* CHARLES) Seems to have been a
             bit of an accident, old girl.

LILY   What happened.

CARDEW   Well, I popped out for a smoke and met
             Longfellow coming in. He said he fancied a
             drag so I gave him the cigar. Next thing I know
             there's an almighty bang and the chap
             disappears. Found his shoes.

LILY   (*to* PRATT) This is your fault!

PRATT   Not entirely.

CARDEW   Might have to decline the war office job, old
             girl. This is all getting a bit much for me
             y'know.

             (LILY *glares at* CARDEW *and hurries out*
             through the hall door with PRATT *following*
             close behind.)

PRATT   (*as he exits*) He'll be all right. We'll probably
             find him on the roof.

             (CYNTHIA *spots her opportunity and slips out*
             through the secret panel, unseen by CARDEW.
             CARDEW *glances round and sees that the room*
             is now empty. He puts the shoes down, closes
             the hall door and turns, looking around the
             room. He begins to laugh theatrically, rising
             to a crescendo before settling to a self
             satisfied, cunning smile.)

CARDEW   (*theatrically in his normal voice*) There is a
             tide in the affairs of men, which, taken at the
             flood, leads on to fortune. On such a full sea

are we now afloat, and we must take the current when it serves, or lose our ventures.

(Cardew *starts to laugh theatrically again. He looks around the room. A sudden movement in the dining room attracts his attention. He moves towards the dining room door, calling into the dining room.*)

CARDEW   (*Impersonating* CHARLES *again*) Who's there?

WOMAN   (*off*) It's me, Charles.

CARDEW   Who? Can't quite see you in the shadows there ... there, that's better. (*Uncertain, taking a step backwards.*) I think you should put that down. Do I know you?

WOMAN   (*off*) You should do, Charles. I *am* your wife.

(*The lights fade as the curtain closes.*)

7 8 11 07